BOUDOIRS to BROTHELS

The Intimate World of Wild West Women

BY MICHAEL RUTTER

GW00578149

FARCOUNTRY
PRESS

THANKS TO ROSEMARY LARKIN.

ISBN: 978-1-56037-600-2

For more information about our books, write Farcountry Press, P.O. Box 5630, Helena, MT 59604; call (800) 821-3874; or visit www.farcountrypress.com.

Library of Congress Cataloging-in-Publication Data

Rutter, Michael, 1953-
  Boudoirs to brothels : the intimate world of Wild West women / by Michael Rutter.
    pages cm
  Includes bibliographical references and index.
  ISBN 978-1-56037-600-2 -- ISBN 1-56037-600-7
  1. Prostitutes--West (U.S.)--Biography. 2. Brothels--West
(U.S.)--History--19th century. 3. Frontier and pioneer life--West (U.S.)
4. West (U.S.)--History--19th century. 5. West (U.S.)--Biography. I.
Title.
  F590.5.R864 2014
  306.740820978--dc23
                          2014011926

 Produced and printed in the United States of America.

24 23 22 21 20   3 4 5 6 7

TABLE OF CONTENTS

INTRODUCTION

Somewhere between starvation and physical abuse, between venereal disease and suicide, between social alienation and depression, falls the woman of easy virtue. She might have been a parlor courtesan, a dance hall girl in a saloon, or a streetwalker. Perhaps she was a painted lady in a workingman's brothel, a hooker in a high-volume crib house—or the lowest of all, a whore at a "hog ranch." A few women joined the sisterhood to try and make big money; too many felt they had no other option.

One woman, a German immigrant, lost her husband and family in a cholera epidemic while going overland. She was rescued by another wagon train and dropped off at the nearest town. She spoke no English and had nowhere to turn. Within weeks, she was making her living as a high-volume prairie queen, doing forty or fifty men in a long evening. Most of the men were love-starved cowboys off a trail drive. To dull the shame, she drank cheap whiskey until her head buzzed. If money was tight, she took tablespoons of laudanum until she was numb. The half-drunk men she serviced were too anxious to take off their boots or spurs. If she was not too far under the effects of the whiskey or laudanum, she remembered to stretch a rain slicker over the bottom of her bed to catch the mud and manure from her clients' boots. This kept their boots from soiling the bedding and their spurs from scratching the bedposts.

Sadly, little is known about the working girls in the American West. Society labeled them as fallen and did its best to sweep them under the table along with the other social misfits. In the nineteenth century, the establishment simply wasn't interested in recording their stories or writing ethnographies about their profession. These women were consumable products who were used and discarded. Until recently, they rarely warranted more than a mention in historical documents. In retrospect, we've come to realize their stories are worth telling and are an important part of our heritage. Ladies of the evening, beyond the war paint and the come-ons, were, after all, human beings. Beyond the haze of whiskey and opium and the smell of unwashed men, they were women and girls who had fears and hopes and aspirations. They had mothers and fathers and sisters and brothers. Like all human beings, they hoped for something better, for love and security, but they were constricted by their profession. They were, after all, "sinners," the artificers, the practitioners of venal arts, but they knew too keenly how difficult it was to escape the conventions of their social and economic prisons.

There was a saying among working girls: "You can look homeward, honey, but you can never go back again." It seemed that a whore by any other name was still a whore, and society was slow to forgive a fallen sister. If a woman made a wrong turn, she was not only dead to the community, she was dead to her family. As a madam who recruited runaway girls for her brothel casually observed, "you befriend her"—feed her a square meal, slip her some laudanum, and get her with a man. From that point, "she's with you from then on." She can't go home anymore—and she wouldn't even if she were able. She's ruined. The madam knew it, and the girl knew it.

The ethos of the times formulated a rigid distinction between a *good* and a *bad* woman. While it seems an oversimplification by modern considerations, there was an imaginary line that one could not cross without dire consequences. It placed a woman on one side or the other of an unyielding morality. Plainly stated, you were either good or you were not. It was as one-sided as that. The question of a woman's virtue was black or white. A decent woman was a creature to be honored and respected. She had virtue and was the embodiment of womanhood. She was the wife, the sister, the mother, and the daughter.

Because of her moral choices, a fallen angel must therefore be a bad woman. She was the whore, the lady of the evening, or the shady lady who had forfeited her greatest gifts for thirty pieces of silver. She had lost her God-given rights to be a *true* woman. Indeed, so potent were a good woman's powers, some argued her virtue would keep her from getting a venereal disease if her husband strayed. Like the fallen angels of heaven, a prostitute had chosen darkness while standing in the light and was thus

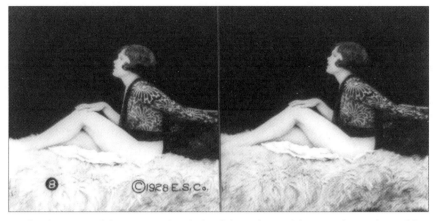

Under the mores of the times, only a lady of the night would pose so brazenly, and for a stereoscopic viewer no less. COURTESY LIBRARY OF CONGRESS, LC-USZ62-95618.

a social pariah, a moral leper. She was unfit to associate with decent folk. She corrupted the morals of weaker men, men who naturally fell prey to her siren call. She was a "public" woman who had slid from grace by giving up her precious morality. Her choices also cost her many of her civil rights. In western towns, it was difficult for a so-called "common" woman to have the law treat her fairly or give her due cause. For this reason, it was nearly impossible to prove a rape or a physical assault charge if you were a prostitute. In the eyes of the law, such a woman was hardly a citizen. And because she was "common," how could rape be an issue?

A man had moral latitude and a handy double standard working in his favor. By his nature and gender, society felt he was more venal, like Father Adam, and thus more prone to the carnal flirtations and the seductive machinations of fallen Eves. A man stumbling was at least understandable, if not predictable, especially in boomtowns where men outnumbered women several hundred to one. Prostitutes were welcomed in boomtowns as a necessary service. It was a given that men left to their own devices made poor moral choices. However, as towns grew and developed, and decent women started to populate the physical and cultural landscape, bawdy women didn't go away but were shamed and "placed" in the unseen corners. It was understood that with the help of a good woman, men could be brought back under control. A good woman could reverse a man's natural proclivity toward the carnal, sensual, and devilish and fight to keep him on that straight and narrow path.

Western women were proactive, being the first in the United States to win the vote. They did more than talk about reform at tea parties. They fought to clean up their towns and rid their communities of the moral vices they felt threatened their families. City fathers paid public lip service to feminine protestations for decency, but these men were also pragmatists. They knew that taxes, licenses, and fines from prostitutes (as well as other sin taxes) were a significant part of a municipality's revenue. For example, in Wyoming public education was funded largely by prostitution. Leaders periodically arrested, jailed, or sent prostitutes out of town "on a rail" as an act of good faith, paying lip service to calls for moral purity, but it was a delicate political balance. To placate the good women of the town, many communities developed an out-of-sight out-of-mind policy. They created "sin" districts, often called the red light district, the line, the tenderloin district, or the other side of the tracks, so decent folk could avoid associations with the fallen. Prostitution didn't go away, of course, but it retreated to the back alleys in the seedy parts of town.

Boudoirs to Brothels is a book about this shadowy group of women who lived in a netherworld on the dark edge of traditional morality. Before towns relegated the oldest profession to prescribed zones, a prostitute on the street was required to look down as she walked. Because of her status, society had not granted her the right to look directly at decent folk. Under no circumstances was she allowed to address or converse with a so-called decent woman. Any complaint or infraction could result in a fine, jail time, or a stage ticket out of town. In some towns, respectable women would stay home during prescribed times each week, so prostitutes could shop without infecting their sensibilities.

Searching for the real stories behind these women is a difficult task. Amid the clichés, the folklore, and the legends, threads of truth give us a curious insight into this most secretive of professions. Like mountain men, prostitutes were noted for hyperbole and tall tales. Their professional lives were seemingly open books—which they felt was good for business. They were, after all, common women whom anyone could buy. They used monikers and hyperbole as a business card: Squirrel Tooth Alice, the Queen of the Underworld, the Queen of the Blondes, or Big Nose Kate. They spun stories and mythologies about themselves that were told and retold, even to this day. Such tales are interesting, but they reveal little about the real person. Personal lives were kept private to protect what shreds of dignity they had left and to protect their family's reputation. They were public women, sold to the highest bidder, but that was their working persona. They revealed little about who they really were—and at the time no one cared. In this book, we certainly look at the myths and folklore behind these fascinating women. But more important, we'll explore who these women really were when they washed off their war paint. ⇒

CHAPTER ONE

MADAM DORA DUFRAN

The Black Hills Madam

A rguably, Madam Dora was the most notorious madam in the Dakotas, if not the most colorful. Without question, she was the most successful. Dora did business in an age when prospectors made fortunes overnight, and angry men settled arguments with single-action Colts. Lakota warriors roamed the plains, making travel perilous, while buffalo hunters plied their trade on the diminishing herds. In 1874, Custer's Black Hills Expedition discovered gold near present-day Custer, South Dakota. It was frontpage news around the world. The discovery went viral, blowing the lid off an obscure stretch of mountains the Lakota called *Paha Sapa*, "the heart of it all." Tragically, the discovery would sound the death knell for the nomadic Sioux's traditional way of life. To complicate the equation, in 1875 a large placer deposit was found in a gulch some folks called Deadwood. The newspapers advised it might be the strike of the century. The narrow Deadwood Gulch became a thriving boomtown almost overnight. Perhaps 5,000 would-be miners stormed the fledgling town as quickly as they could board a ship, catch a train, or mount a horse. Never mind that the strike was technically on lands granted to the Lakota during the Treaty of Laramie in 1868.

The Tragedy of Calamity Jane

In the late nineteenth and early twentieth centuries, Calamity Jane (Martha Jane Canary) was the unquestioned heroine of pulp fiction and dime novels. While galloping her horse, she could shoot a match head from a man's clenched jaw, rescue a baby on a mountain road before a runaway stage went over a cliff, or show up to fight off some marauding Indians and save a wagon train of pioneers. She was an unorthodox woman of the West who could do a man's work. Calamity wore men's clothing and carried guns. Her feats were nonpareil. This frontier woman could skin a team of mules and ride a wild mustang. In print, she was a hard-riding, hard-drinking, and quick-shooting woman. She would cuss and swear, but she was a defender of truth and righteousness.

Calamity Jane was one of the most famous women in the American West. She was the darling of the Eastern press and pulp fiction. Unfortunately, she shared little of the profits, often resorting to shoplifting to survive. COURTESY LIBRARY OF CONGRESS, IMAGE LC-USZ62-47390.

The true story of Calamity Jane, however, was the antithesis of her fictional persona. Martha Jane's real life was colorful, but it was closer to a tragedy than an adventure novel. Her story is clouded by folklore and mythology, but she's one of the few women in the West we can get a focused picture of if we do a little digging. The real Calamity was the sort who would buy drinks for the house, but she was also a low-end prostitute (a crib girl), a drunk, a vagabond, and a blowhard. She was loud and obnoxious when she was drinking. Whatever money she earned as a show woman, whether she worked for Buffalo Bill or other Western projects, was quickly drunk or lost gambling. Because she had such a problem with alcohol and was so belligerent when drinking, she never stayed employed long. This was unfortunate since several of her business opportunities could have set her up for life. Mostly, Martha Jane was impoverished and regularly went to bed hungry. She struggled to keep a roof over her head and resorted to selling her body to stay alive. Most of her prostitution experiences were in low-end cribs or houses where the men were desperate and the prices were cheap. In spite of her tabloid persona, prostitution was her go-to profession. Calamity Jane mostly lost when she gambled, but the real monkey on her back was drink. She had been an alcoholic for decades. This was a far cry from the Calamity Jane written about in papers and in dime novels.

She had a streak of feminism and independence long before such things were fashionable, but she also had a secret desire to be a wife and have a happy home with children. She invented her relationship with Wild Bill Hickok, also fabricating that he was the father of her child. Naturally, Wild Bill wasn't able to set the story straight because he was dead when Jane spread the rumor. She was considered a homely woman in her day. In many of the pictures we have of her, she was in men's clothing. This was in part to perpetuate her image for writers and journalists, since she actually preferred a dress to pants and a wool shirt. She swore like a cowboy and was a tolerably good shot (although not the crack shot of legend). She was uncomfortable in all the traditional roles she was asked to play, never doing one thing or staying in one place for long.

Calamity Jane was a personal friend of Dora DuFran, and an inveterate vagabond and alcoholic who occasionally supported herself by working as a low-end prostitute.
COURTESY LIBRARY OF CONGRESS, IMAGE LC-USZ62-47389.

Men from every walk of life, all looking to make their fortunes, poured into the Hills, searching for their own piece of El Dorado. Life might have been cheap in a gold camp, but nothing else was. All supplies had to be shipped by wagon or mule train, including the working girls. Such a trip was fraught with danger and difficulty, especially from the war-like Sioux eager to chase the white man out of the heart of their sacred homeland. In 1876, a renowned plainsman named Charlie Utter realized that it was more profitable supplying prospectors than to do the actual digging and panning. He led a wagon train to Deadwood with all the essentials of life—whiskey, tobacco, dry goods, and, of course, women with a fancy price tag. Stocking the prospectors was the surest way to turn a dollar. Mining at best was a risky business.

When Charlie's long-awaited train rolled into town, a young woman named Madam Dora DuFran, along with her denizen competitors, Madam Dirty Em and Madame Moustache, reportedly looked over the new recruits. Each madam tried to convince the most alluring young trollops to work in her respective house. Thousands of men were running loose in Deadwood, and more were coming from all parts of the earth. Never mind the thousands who came in from their claims and mines to blow off steam on weekends. The man-to-woman ratio was well over a hundred to one. Truthfully, a madam or a working girl didn't have to be all that choosy. Even Calamity Jane, who was—well, there's no way to say it politely—quite ugly, made a living in Deadwood's houses of sin. Nevertheless, Dora DuFran was said to have the prettiest girls in her house. She ran a nice brothel and would naturally attract the top working girls.

This cherished story has been told and retold with great delight, but is it factual? We know Charlie Utter's famous wagon train came to Deadwood with supplies and probably with working girls. But was Madam Dora there to meet it? Those who enthusiastically spun this bit of DuFran mythology might have been a bit challenged with basic ciphering—maybe they had one too many tin cups of red-eye before story time. According to the birth date on her headstone, which reads 1868, Dora would have been around eight or nine years old when Utter's train of supplies, whiskey, and tarts hit the gulch in 1876. That's certainly a bit young for a madam, even by Deadwood standards. Still, we can't completely trust Dora's reckoning either. She was a bit vain about things like her age. She could have fudged when she gave her birth date. If she wasn't born in 1868, as she claimed, Dora was probably born in the mid-1860s. Either way, she probably missed the Utter wagon train entirely. Even a strapping fourteen-year-old madam was unlikely— possible, but not probable. The legend makes a great frontier tall tale. This also hints at one of the major problems a historian has collecting stories of this nature. There are more myths than facts. To make life interesting, the labyrinth of myth and lore is full of contradictions—and so are the facts.

At some point, Dora did come to Deadwood, and probably at a tender age. She likely worked as a dancehall girl and a prostitute, but it's also true that she became a successful madam at a young age. We're simply not sure when these life and career changes took place. And yes, Dora and her establishment did have a reputation for being honest with her girls and fair with the men who patronized her place. She hired pretty girls and prided herself on having the best-dressed whores on the Northern Plains. Dora also insisted that her employees washed often—something one could not count on in a western town. She demanded cleanliness from her employees. She also insisted that her girls be friendly and pleasant to all patrons no matter how they acted. It was one of the reasons why she was not only the most successful madam in the territory, but in the entire West, too. Dora's brothel prospered, and she opened successful houses across what is now South Dakota—like fast-food joints franchising into new towns. The cathouse business was a competitive, cut-throat market, but Dora was convinced that customer service and good business practices would keep her houses profitable, and she was right. Her brothel in Deadwood had been more successful than she'd imagined, so she branched out to other parts of South Dakota, establishing businesses in Belle Fourche, Sturgis, Lead, Rapid City, and even to Miles City, Montana. She had a knack for knowing when an area was going to grow, and she was there to capitalize on the development.

Madam DuFran was not the cold-hearted madam we often read about in frontier tales. Legend and fact both point out that Dora was kind and considerate. She paid her girls well and didn't cheat them or steal their tips. There are also tales about her grubstaking a miner, cattleman, or rancher— or a man simply down on his luck. She was quick with a meal for a hungry

Dora DuFran was one of the most colorful women, if not one of the most successful madams, in Western history. She was a clever businesswoman and made her South Dakota establishments very lucrative.

COURTESY DEADWOOD HISTORY, ADAMS MUSEUM COLLECTION, DEADWOOD, SD.

man or a destitute family. Frontier stories have exploded into mythology, so they are hard to unravel, but enough are based in fact to give us a picture of her charitable character. When it came to the bawdy trade and whorehouse whiskey, she would gladly take a man's money for services rendered. But she also wouldn't turn away the hungry, and she was generous with charitable causes.

Her full name was Amy Helen Dorothea Bolsaw. "Dora" was her family nickname as well as her professional name. She was born in Liverpool, England, supposedly in 1868. Her family relocated to Bloomfield, New Jersey, when Dora was a small child. Not satisfied with his situation and wanting to grab a slice of the American dream, her father uprooted his family again and headed west to what he hoped was the Promised Land. He ended up near Lincoln, Nebraska. He wanted land and was infatuated with the vastness of the American prairie, but the life of a pioneer family was never easy. Young Dora had inherited some of her father's drive, and at an early age, she, too, dreamed of wealth and success. A comely girl, she flowered into a beautiful young woman. She wanted nothing to do with dirty fingernails, drought, and crop failure. She saw her mother age before her eyes as she raised children and chickens, cooked meals, tended the garden, milked cows, and helped her husband in the fields. Dora Bolsaw thought of bright lights and pretty clothes. She would soon learn of a shortcut to what she assumed would be an easier life through the gold and silver ready for the taking in a man's pockets.

She was a clever girl with a country education, but she wasn't a fool. She realized that entrepreneurial opportunities for women on the plains were few. She noticed, too, the effect that she had on the men and boys around her, and by the time she was fourteen, she had reportedly entered into the bawdy profession. She likely resented that a man could easily better himself, but a woman had few choices and on her own faced a life of poverty. For her, like other women in her trade, even with the inherent dangers of prostitution, the sporting life seemed the best way for an aspiring girl to seek her fortune. It's unlikely that her parents would have approved. Perhaps she ran away from home. We know almost nothing about this phase of her life. After all, a young prostitute rarely writes home about her profession. For being so famous and flamboyant, precious few details exist to reveal the secrets of her life. She probably intended it to be that way, so she could protect her family's good name (her parents lived into the twentieth century, and she was very protective of them). Dora did, however, understand men and knew their passions could be a ticket to prosperity. Dora knew, too, that men found her beautiful. She started as a whore, but she had no desire to be a working prostitute for long—the money was too little and the risk too much when one was a common bawd. She wanted an easier life than her mother's, but she wanted an easier life than a working girl's, too. She didn't want to worry about losing the farm or if she could feed her family. She wanted to drink champagne and laugh and let her girls receive the gentleman callers while she ran the business.

Dora had a charming personality, and in spite of her profession, she entertained some respectability in the community. Even more interesting, Dora was one of the few women who appears to have enjoyed a successful marriage in spite of her vocation. When she was a young whore, she met a dashing man named Joseph DuFran. Sparks flew, and they fell in love, the whore and the gambler. Even more of an anomaly, the young couple seemed to stay in love throughout their lives. Joseph not only supported her in her bawdy profession, he helped her build it. She had ambitions to make a lot of money, and with his help, it happened. Unfortunately, we know little about Joseph. Happy marriages are very rare—or lasting—in this profession. It's an occupation loaded with baggage. Joseph gambled a little, but not to excess. Like his wife, he had a good mind for business. His life revolved around his wife, gambling, and running the family business, which he did behind the scenes. Dora was the front woman and in charge of the girls and the customers, while Joseph managed the books, did the purchasing, and presumably was the bouncer.

At the age of forty-seven, in 1909, Joseph died. His death broke Dora's heart. He was buried in the Mount Moriah Cemetery in Deadwood. As a point of interest, her beloved pet parrot, Fred, was buried in the family plot, too. When Dora finally went to her reward some twenty-five years after Joseph, the family was reunited—man, woman, and parrot.

The inscription on her headstone read, not without irony, "A Noted Social Worker."

The Three Mile Hog Ranch at Fort Laramie

The Three Mile Hog Ranch was a couple of miles away from Fort Laramie and may be the only hog ranch listed on the National Register of Historic Places. The proprietors were two businessmen by the names of Adolph Cuny and Jules Ecoffey. They started Three Mile as a trading post and a watering hole in 1873. They sold supplies and watered-down drinks, but they looked for greater profits. The next year, they built eight small, two-room cabins (often called cribs) and brought in ten business girls to attract soldiers from the nearby military post. As their success grew, they added barns, a bar, a billiard hall, shops, and corrals. Building continued until 1885.

Three Mile maintained legitimate business trade throughout its expansion. In 1876, the Black Hills Stage Company and the Cheyenne Stage Company used Three Mile as an inn for stage passengers to hold over.

Three Mile earned a reputation as a wild, sinful place: cards, whiskey, and sleazy women. It offered anything to separate a soldier from his pay. It was reported that Martha Jane Canary (sometimes spelled Cannary), better known as Calamity Jane, was an off-and-on crib girl for Three Mile Hog Ranch.

Her most popular bawdy house was, surprisingly, not in Deadwood, but in Belle Fourche on Fifth Avenue. The street was filled with vices of every kind, from gambling joints to saloons and whorehouses. Saloons literally lined the street, so residents simply called it Saloon Street. The upstairs rooms over the saloons were filled with brothels and other types of vice. There was a lot of competition in the bawdy business, but that never bothered Dora. She made her establishment the best place in town. Belle Fourche was a good move for Dora. Deadwood had changed from a wild and woolly boomtown to a mining community. Belle Fourche was a thriving cow center, and that meant a lot of lonely cowboys. The town was an ideal site located at the forks of the Belle Fourche, Redwater, and Haycreek Rivers. There was plenty of water. But just as important, the Freemont,

In the early 1890s, Belle Fourche was little more than a few buildings located at the forks of the Belle Fourche, Redwater, and Haycreek Rivers. The town soon became one of the largest cattle shipping towns in the United States. Belle Fourche was the home of Dora DuFran's most successful house. COURTESY SOUTH DAKOTA STATE HISTORICAL SOCIETY.

Elkhorn, and Missouri Valley Railroad could move livestock from the ranches and rangeland. Plus, the railroads planned to expand west, opening up more markets. Almost overnight Belle Fourche grew into one of the more important cattle and sheep distribution centers in the West (as it still is today). In the mid-1890s, as many as 8,000 cars of beef were shipped out of town in one season. The town, known as the "Beautiful Fork," was the Wild West all over. For Dora's line of work, it was the mother lode.

Her establishment on Saloon Street was known as Diddlin' Dora's. She called her place the Three Ds (Dining, Drinking, and Dancing), and jokingly referred to her house as a place you could bring your mother. Even so, as one patron said, "I sure wouldn't want to bring my mother here." Belle Fourche was a cattle boomtown with more staying power than a precarious mining community. Whiskey flowed like water, a summer's wages were lost in a few hands of poker, and morals were loose and easy. When the cowboys came into town, the girls not occupied in their upstairs brothel would stand at the windows or on the balconies and shout, hoping to attract business. This was something that Dora, or any other madam for that matter, encouraged. The painted ladies would wave and sometimes make lewd gestures at the trail-weary cowhands eager for the drive to end. It was not uncommon for the women to throw garters, bits of clothing, even underwear at the lonely punchers to attract their attention while stirring up primordial urges. In return, if a cowboy saw a girl he liked, he threw up his hat, and she caught it. The cowboy might tie up his horse and go up and transact business. More likely, he would go back to his job and get the herd settled, penned, or sold. Then he'd clean up, maybe have a bath and buy some new clothes, have a few drinks, and head back to the girl who had his hat. After his business was transacted with her, he'd grab his hat and go on his way.

Another interesting aspect of Dora DuFran was her association with Calamity Jane. Their lives crossed paths a number of times. It was reported that Calamity worked as a prostitute in one of Madam DuFran's broth-els until she could get financially settled. This could be true, although Calamity Jane was more of a "hog ranch" girl. Her style was working low-end places near army camps and forts, not as a parlor girl. Maybe Dora was being nice. She had known Calamity Jane (Martha Jane Canary) when Deadwood was a prospering boomtown. The two were good friends, and Dora was one of the few people who readily understood Calamity and accepted her unconditionally. Dora knew Jane had a good heart, but she also knew that Calamity Jane was a loud, ugly drunk who was, at best, self-destructive. Jane squandered her money and was usually broke and impoverished. She told extravagant stories that were far from the truth, but they were readily published and accepted as fact by gullible readers. Her legend was larger than life, but she was more like a deer in the head-lights, often taken advantage of by the media, which was eager for a quick quote or a story. More than once Jane was near starving. She worked in the lowest houses and shoplifted in general stores to survive.

In 1903, Dora's friend Jane, who had been worn out by life and exces-sive alcohol consumption, came to Dora's brothel at Belle Fourche. Dora always had time for Calamity Jane. And there was always a place for her to stay, even a job if she wanted it. She was very ill. All she had to show for her life was a ragged travel case and a few clothes. Dora, of course, took care of her and hired Calamity Jane to do laundry and cook for the girls. Later, Martha Jane left for the last time. She died not long after. The press

The Temperance movement sought reforms beyond Prohibition, targeting gambling, prostitution, and other vices as well. Here, Temperance workers rally in Miller, South Dakota. COURTESY SOUTH DAKOTA STATE HISTORICAL SOCIETY.

had a field day, printing all sorts of mythical fabrications about the wild life of Calamity Jane. As her friend, Dora wanted to tell her story and try to balance the media exaggerations.

In a no-holds-barred vignette entitled the *Low Down on Calamity Jane*, Dora defended Martha Jane Canary vigorously from the exaggerated stories in newspapers and pulps under the byline of D. Dee. ". . . [S]he was not brought up with every protection from the evils of the world and with good associates. . . . [She] was a product of the wild and wooly west. She was not immoral; but unmoral. She took more on her shoulders than most women could. She performed many hundreds of deeds of kindness and received very little pay."

Dora was a loyal friend.

In 1909, Dora moved to Rapid City. She needed a change, and this was a good place for business. While Belle Fourche was her best house, with the advent of Prohibition, Dora's venture in Rapid City was a sound business move and proved quite lucrative. She could charge inflated prices for her liquor. Dora worked hard and enjoyed continued financial success, although she missed Joseph.

The Rapid City brothel birthed one particularly interesting episode, when a heavy flood marooned a number of the city's most prosperous businessmen in Dora's place of business. The wives of the men in question were worried that their menfolk might be swept away in the flood. However, these women soon found out their husbands had been spending time at Dora's and couldn't get across the water. They became very angry. To further strain domestic tranquility, said businessmen had to spend another night in the infamous whorehouse because they were cut off by the floodwaters. After the flood receded, the men in question were apparently attacked with rolling pins, cooking utensils, sticks, or whatever was handy . . . and cold shoulders. Forgiveness was a long time coming.

In her sixties, Dora started to slow down and was feeling poorly. On August 5, 1934, at the age of sixty-six, she died of heart failure. Her body was taken to Deadwood where she was buried next to her beloved husband and her parrot, Fred. ⇒

CHAPTER TWO

LIBBY THOMPSON

Squirrel Tooth Alice

B efore she was known as Squirrel Tooth Alice, the eccentric madam of the southwest plains, she was known as Mary Elizabeth Haley. Mary Elizabeth, or Libby to her family, was born to privilege in Belton, Texas, on October 18, 1855. At the time, Belton was a thriving frontier town on the Brazos River north of Austin. The soil was fertile, and the cattle were plentiful. Belton was the last point of civilization for those heading west. It was also a feeder city for the northern herds, including those following the Chisholm Trail. Libby's father ran a successful plantation near the banks of the river and was one of the wealthiest men in the area. As a young girl, Libby lacked for little. The Haleys enjoyed a comfortable standard of living even on the edge of a vast wilderness. Outlaws and bandits lived in the no-man's-land beyond the settlement—attacks on travelers and supply trains were all too common. So were Comanche raids on outlying farms and ranches. The braves were especially interested in horses, supplies, and captives. Occasionally, they would raid uncomfortably near Belton. No one, including the Haleys, felt truly at ease; most men went armed.

A quiet Comanche camp belies the reality that violent raids—on other tribes and Euro-American settlers—were an integral part of the tribe's culture.
COURTESY LIBRARY OF CONGRESS, IMAGE LC-USZ62-53778.

While the dangers of a developing town in the Texas wilderness were ever present, in the late 1850s and early 1860s, if Texans were not talking about cotton, cattle, or crops, they were talking about slavery and the right of secession. Political discussions were usually heated, and most Texans favored joining the Confederacy even if they weren't slave holders. When Sam Houston, hero of the Texas Revolution and the Republic of Texas, came to Belton to argue for the Union, he was booed and shouted down. He took out his revolvers and laid them on the podium and called for order. He got through his unpopular message, sort of. Few, if any, supported his pro-Union arguments, even if he was a slave owner. The Confederate firebrand, James Haley, was surely there doing his best to shout down Houston. He was a vocal, if not radical, supporter of slavery and secession. His stubbornness and rebellion would later rub off on his daughter. James' support of the rebellion would eventually cost him his wealth and his land. Financially, he'd never recover from his loyalty to the "cause." He was part of the rea-son that Belton was a Confederate hotspot. The Belton area sent more than 1,000 men to fight for the Gray. We don't know what his part was in some of the local mob violence, but during the war and right after, several Unionists were brought up on bogus charges and hanged from handy oaks.

With so many local men fighting in the war and all the extra sup-plies and money going to the Southern war machine, local defenses around Belton were relaxed. Outlaws were emboldened, and criminal behavior was common. Worse, marauding Comanche parties soon discovered weak-ened defenses as they probed deeper into the developed regions of Texas. Plunder was easy to come by. The tribes were angry, naturally, with the encroachment of whites into their homeland and decimation of the buf-falo herds. The War Between the States provided ample opportunity for revenge. The Comanche embraced raiding as an important part of their way of life. They showed little mercy in battle and expected none in re-turn. Probably the finest horsemen in the world, they could ride deep into enemy country, strike, and be miles away before a retaliatory party was gathered. In 1864, they raided the Haley plantation. James had lost most of his workforce to the war effort. His money was nearly gone, so he couldn't afford to hire the men he needed to work the plantation—men who would normally help defend his property. His place was easy pickings for the well-disciplined raiders. Among other items of plunder, ten-year-old Libby was kidnapped.

Young Libby's parents were heartbroken, but they were not without hope. Their daughter was young and healthy. There was a good chance she was alive. The Comanche often adopted children or made them slaves. Her parents' worry was finding young Libby before she reached puberty and was married off to a brave. If they could find her, it was usually pos-sible to buy captives back—which is what the Haley family prayed for. They probed various leads and tried to locate their daughter among the many branches of the Comanche tribes. They contacted the Texas Rangers, with whom Haley had some influence. They also spread the word to trap-pers, traders, and buffalo hunters. James Haley knew he was in a race to get his daughter back as soon as he could. The longer the Comanche had Mary Elizabeth, the more difficult it would be. And the more likely she would be ruined. He did not want to see his daughter raped, abused, or married to a savage—any of these acts would be unspeakable and would spoil her for polite society. He knew that he'd raised Libby to be a proper girl. In Haley's view, it was better for her to die than be deflowered.

After three years of searching, it appeared hopeless, and then, against all hope, in 1867, Libby was found and ransomed. Her father was sure it had been too long. When he saw his daughter, who was no longer a child but a young woman, he knew the worst had occurred. She had been defiled. Libby was excited to come home and see her loved ones. However, the warm welcome she likely dreamed of did not occur. Instead, she received a cold shoulder from her father. James could see no scars and bruises on her, but what he feared most, he could not see. There was always a prejudice against any female who had been a captive, especially if she was sexually mature. Her father's poisoned attitude spread to her family and to the other settlers in Belton. Soon few would have anything to do with her. Her father could not recommend her for marriage because she was ruined. Libby, like her father, was stubborn and refused to talk about her captivity when he tried to question her.

Libby heard their talk and felt more alone with her own people than she had among the Comanche. Even her neighbors and old friends would avoid speaking to her. Her experience was not uncommon. One famous example was Cynthia Ann Parker, who was kidnapped by a Comanche band at nine. After she was freed, she was so uncomfortable in prejudiced frontier culture that she ran off and found her way back to her old tribe. She married a chief, and her son, Quanah Parker, became arguably the most famous Comanche war chief in history. The fates of females and children captured by tribes (even Daniel Boone's daughter was kidnapped and later recovered) were often decided on a whim. Some were killed, some raped, some made into slaves, but many were married into the tribe and fully accepted as members. Taking captives and making them tribal members helped a tribe build up numbers that might have been lowered by disease or war. If captives adjusted to tribal life, they would be assimilated. Another woman named Millie Durgan lived happily with the Kiowa even when she was given the chance to return to her people. She felt more comfortable among the Indians who accepted her.

Libby had no desire to go back to the Indians, but because of her ordeal, she had a tarnished reputation and was a social pariah among her former friends and the male candidates in the local marriage market. No one wanted "used goods" deflowered by the heathen. Few of her old friends would talk to her, let alone come courting. When she was fourteen, a marriageable age in that time, she fell for an older man who apparently was not bothered by her captivity. It felt good to have someone to talk to, let alone be loved by. Libby was tired of being referred to as a "squaw woman" behind her back. She was excited to introduce her new friend to her parents. She was nervous that he was a little older than the local boys she'd normally associate with, so she decided to tell her father they were already married. The first meeting went poorly, especially for her true love. When her father saw that her intended was at least double her age, he knew the gentleman in question was taking advantage of Libby because of her weakened emotional state. He didn't say anything. He simply pulled out his pistol and shot him in the chest. Libby's lover dropped as dead as a stone on the front porch. Her father felt he was within his rights. Apparently law enforcement officials and the good citizens of Belton agreed with him. There was no reprisal or official inquiry. A father has to do what a father has to do. But so did Libby. She would take no more. She ran away, heading for Kansas and a new life, never to return.

Libby knew she was ruined, although it's unlikely she left home with the intention of becoming a prostitute; she left home to start a new life. She ended up in a dance hall where she danced and worked as a prostitute. Abilene was a cow town with all the rough edges and plenty of lonely men off the trail drives who wanted to be entertained. She met a young cowhand in the saloon named William Thompson, known as "Texas Billy." He was the brother of the famous Texas gunman Ben Thompson. Texas Billy was considered a first-rate cowman, but his true love was gambling. When his luck was bad, he hired on with trail herds. In his spare time he tested Lady Luck. Billy and Libby set up house together, but it was a loose arrangement. Libby danced, whirling about and showing her ankles— even a flash of her leg. She also sold herself and shared the takings with Thompson, so he could gamble. Billy, at least in the first years of their relationship, wasn't bothered by sharing his affections as long as he got part of the hourly rate. They moved from town to town as their whims dictated. Sometimes they made good money, but since Libby liked to chase Lady Luck, too, they were often broke.

They were living in sin, but they tried to be respectable. They told everyone they were married. It was legal for her to be a prostitute, but in many towns it was illegal for her to live with a man outside of marriage. During the hard times Texas Billy would take a job ramrodding a herd of cattle. Libby worked in dance halls and sold her favors. In 1873 a pregnant Libby followed him on the drive. Ordinarily, a woman would not be allowed to accompany a cowhand on the trail, but because Billy was the boss, she rode in the wagon. On the trail she gave birth to their first son. When the trail drive was over, they married and made their union legal. During their twenty-four-year relationship, she gave birth to nine children (at least six were Billy's). Neither of the two proved to be good parents. Both were more interested in gambling and honky-tonks and drinking than rearing children. Libby spent little time at home, and Billy was gone on gambling trips or pushing cattle on drives.

Eventually, they ended up in Sweetwater, Texas, and thought about putting down roots. They bought a ranch outside of town and a dance hall (complete with gambling, saloon, and whorehouse). The group of girls that Libby managed was the most lucrative of all their enterprises. She was a gambler, but she was also a good businesswoman. They were happy to be settled and out of Kansas where Billy had run afoul of the law. During an all-night drinking binge, a drunken Billy triggered a fatal piece of lead into Ellsworth County Sheriff Chauncey Whitney. He was thrown in jail, but he claimed the shooting was an accident. Nevertheless, Chauncey had been a popular man, and there was talk of an old-fashioned lynching. Billy's cattle company bailed him out, and Billy was no fool. He skipped out, making his way to Texas—not trusting his young neck to the outcome of a Kansas trial. In 1876, a couple of Texas Rangers with a warrant caught up with him and sent him back to Kansas. He stood trial, sweating that he would not make it out alive. To his good fortune, the shooting was ruled an accident, so he was freed and rode like hell out of town.

Billy and Libby were well known among cattle towns on the southern plains. In Dodge City, Kansas, for example, Libby was well appreciated for

The Realities of Prostitution: Children

One of the realities of prostitution was children—children who were often unwanted, neglected, and unkempt. Past the lights and glitter, past the men who didn't linger, past the alcohol and drugs, past mothers worn out and hung over, shabby children played in alleys and on streets late into the night. Too many were hungry, and a number would become orphans. Selling one's body wasn't a good profession for motherhood.

Obviously, most prostitutes did what they could to avoid pregnancy. Childbirth was dangerous, but it also meant time out from her profession and making a living, a living that was at best tenuous. Plus there was the added burden of taking care of and rearing a child. Most birth control practices were home remedies and ineffective. Some venereal diseases might render a woman sterile, but pregnancy was always a fear. If pregnant, some women tried home methods to abort the fetus, although such methods were usually ineffectual. Others sought an abortion from a doctor or a purveyor of the practice. Such procedures were not without risk.

A string of children was most common outside crib houses and shabbier brothels. More successful women could afford to farm out their children and thus isolate them from their "fallen" lives. Children living at a whorehouse would not be readily accepted into public schools or polite society. There was too much prejudice. If a child was allowed into school, he or she might endure cruel teasing by the other children. Add to this the instability of the profession. A woman would by necessity be forced to travel, which would make securing an education difficult.

The future of such children was tenuous at best. Some gratefully escaped and made normal lives for themselves. Some were educated. Most girls, however, followed their mothers into the trade, making it a family affair, usually at an early age. The boys often found better opportunities, but many entered honky-tonk and dance hall life as a barkeep or a bouncer—it was the only life they knew.

Life could be harsh for a child born to a prostitute. He or she might have no access to socializing with other children, schooling, or health care.
COURTESY LIBRARY OF CONGRESS, IMAGE LC-DIG-NCLC-01953.

Libby Thompson, who worked under the alias of Alice, kept prairie dogs as pets, which led to her distinctive nickname. COURTESY KANSAS STATE HISTORICAL SOCIETY.

her venal arts and Billy as a gambler and a ramrod for a cattle herd. They knew Wyatt Earp and probably met the other Earp brothers, Doc Holliday, Wild Bill Hickok, and Bat Masterson. Libby was good at her job, maybe too good. In the early days, her profession didn't bother Billy. As they grew older together, her past started to haunt him. Each would take separate lovers, and even though several of her children were not fathered by Billy, they somehow managed to come back to one another and try, once again, to mesh their unorthodox lives. Libby was popular with her patrons and handy at managing a string of temperamental bawdy girls.

She probably got her famous moniker in Dodge because Libby Thompson apparently had a fondness for prairie dogs. She thought they were cute and made good pets. She frequently had one or two of the chubby rodents with her in the dance hall, brothel, or saloon—wherever she was working. She liked taking one of her little prairie pups out of its cage, letting it crawl over her as she fondled the creature. She'd scratch its nose and chin and feed it treats like a spoiled lap dog. She had little collars made at the harness shop and trained the dogs to pull tiny carts. She'd even walk them on a leash. The prairie dog shtick was a big attraction and part of her persona. To one particular half-drunken man, starved for the sight of a woman, it was an endearing part of the dance hall/whorehouse experience. Libby, going by the professional name of Alice at the time, was apparently fondling one of her pets. The man in question was on the downward side of a bottle of red-eye. A prairie dog and squirrel must have started looking a lot alike. He found it endearing to watch a beautiful woman giving that little creature her attention. The drunken man noticed Libby (Alice) had a noticeable gap in her front teeth—and that her teeth were slightly bucked. He called her Squirrel Tooth Alice. The name stuck. From then on, Libby's patrons called her Squirrel Tooth Alice. It was done in affection, and she enjoyed the moniker. Plus it was good for business. The name would follow her across the frontier until the end of her career. Perhaps she helped perpetuate the name herself, whispering it into the man's ear and having him spread it about. We're not sure, but she would not have been above doing it.

Wherever she set up shop, she had prairie dogs as pets and was defensive of them. She would tolerate no one hurting or teasing her babies—

who certainly were better cared for than her own children. According to legend, one evening, Squirrel Tooth was worn out after a hard day and was a little cranky. A man who had had too many beers, and was about to see double, was at the cage pestering the porky, overfed pets. What was he thinking? He started to tease one of the creatures, and then he started to poke it with a stick until it squealed. Alice saw him and marched across the room from the bar. Fire burned in her lovely eyes. Everyone in the house knew her dogs were off-limits. She stood in front of the drunk and told him to leave her pets alone. Ignoring her, the man poked them again as if Alice weren't there. She reached into her purse and pulled out a small revolver and pointed it at the man's head. She pulled back the hammer and cocked the weapon. This was enough for the man to discover a bit of common sense and sober up (a cocked handgun at your head will do that). He sheepishly made his way out of the dance hall and never returned.

In the mid-1890s, Billy went on a gambling trip into the mining towns of Colorado to drum up some extra money. Libby stayed in Sweetwater and minded the family enterprises. Billy contracted a serious ailment. It was either consumption or an acute stomach problem. He traveled back to Sweetwater to recover. He was critically ill. Libby realized she did not have the skill or the fortitude to care for him in his last days. She put him on the stage and sent him to his family in southern Texas. She stayed in Sweetwater, and Billy died in 1897.

Libby continued to work until she was a senior citizen.

Libby Thompson, aka Squirrel Tooth Alice, finally retired from the dance hall/whore business in 1921 at the age of sixty-six. She was bold about her profession and never apologized about what she did for a living. She said she was "One . . . who squirms in the night." Indifferent as a parent, her daughters followed her into the bawdy profession. Most of her sons ended up on the wrong side of the law. As one of her daughters commented, "She wasn't average." Her last days were spent in a rest home in California. She died at the ripe old age of ninety-eight. ⇥

CHAPTER THREE

LYDIA TAYLOR

From Under the Lid . . .
Feminist, Prostitute, Author

It seems strange, even to myself, in reviewing my past, that I could have lived through it all, retaining my senses, and to some extent my self pride, still clinging to life and hope, as does the ship-wrecked mariner, longing and craving for something quite different from anything I have known. (Chapter 1, From Under the Lid.)

In 1913, a forty-year-old working prostitute name Lydia Taylor wrote a fascinating personal history entitled *From Under the Lid: An Appeal to True Womanhood*. Her story is a candid reflection of both her personal and professional life as she muses over twenty years in the bawdy business. *From Under the Lid* is also a condemnation of prostitution and a sizzling castigation of the men who fraternize with sporting women. She also warns mothers and young girls about the dangers of a "fallen" life. Her text is one of the few first-hand glimpses of a prostitute in the late nineteenth century. However, it's a snapshot of her feelings rather than an actual day-to-day journal of a reluctant bawdy girl. Her rants about society and men are telling and at times can be diffuse, but insightful. Because there are so few texts of this nature, Lydia's writings are an important slice of history.

As a woman forced into this profession by impoverished circumstances, she questions how a Christian society could allow a woman to become so destitute and desperate that she would be forced to sell her body simply to stay alive. "The great moral wave throughout the country," she writes, "prompts me to lay open my past; show the cause, effect and prove to the public that much of the harm and immorality in this old world has its inception in the home." In addition to addressing how values should be taught in front of the hearth, Lydia warns of the long-term dangers of child abuse—and how physical abuse when she was a child affected the rest of her life. Her story is frank and forthright, if not haunting, but she can't keep silent any longer. A nagging conscience compels her to come out "from under the lid," a lid that society has tried to close upon her and her fellow inmates. She also speaks of the lid she has tried to close upon herself.

A few historians have wondered if Lydia wrote the work herself or had a ghost writer. After all, they argue, she had only a few years of formal education. Of course, such a hypothesis is speculation. Whether she did or didn't have help with her text (the evidence suggests she wrote it herself), it would be wrong to sell her history short. Mrs. Taylor was a highly intelligent woman, a deep thinker. She painted a picture few prostitutes of the nineteenth century allowed us to see. Either way, her story is compelling for anyone interested in American history, women's rights, or the American West. Her writings reflect her feelings as an abused child, a victim, a whore, a feminist, and a survivor. They also highlight her sympathy for other suffragettes. Lydia discusses her guilt for becoming a prostitute as well as her racial biases (which are alarming to the modern reader—but unfortunately typical of her day). Lydia's writing style is Victorian—her prose is heavy by today's standards and a little cumbersome. Nevertheless, her story shows promise as a writer; it also contains the kinds of contextual errors a beginning writer might make (errors that would or should have been corrected had she employed a competent editor or a ghost writer). As a storyteller, Taylor draws frequent moral conclusions that seem obvious to us in this century. She also begs the emotions and belabors what she considers key arguments. Still, her book is delightful and an honest must-read.

Lydia Taylor was a sensitive farm girl from Kansas. She enjoyed the openness and the freedom of the southern plains. Her vivid imagination ran as unchecked as the rolling hills she roamed. Her memory of the seemingly immeasurable prairie is poetic: "I [sat] watch[ing] the heat waves in the distance rolling and tumbling, and there were fleecy clouds about taking shapes, first a house, then an animal, and ever so many shapes." Young Lydia looked at life with a touch of wonder, like a precocious child from an early Wordsworth poem. She was alive in an intoxicating world. Her life was a wondrous clutch of possibilities as she dreamed about what she might be and the places she might visit. While tending the grazing cattle, she writes, "The horizon seemingly the end of the world, yet in my visions I went out and beyond this to the pretty world of my dreams, where people smiled and children laughed." Lydia's writings and musings hint that she might have been more suited to teaching English literature or being a creative writer—not a woman who made her living faking love on her back. Soon, however, the whimsical girl would taste the harsh realities of life. Specifically, the farm that she loved and that had been wrestled from the buffalo and the nomadic Indians was not fertile. At best it reluctantly yielded a difficult living. More troubling, though, was her parents' physical and verbal abuse. As she started to mature and became more aware of her circumstances, she became more calloused. She comments, "Just think what my feelings are when I hear others mention the pleasant days of their childhood. None of the sweetness of youth was mine." In her book, she talks about her childhood and how she eventually sank into prostitution during her late teenage years. She also discusses her guilt over this choice and how loving parents must guard their children from this kind of life.

Born in 1872, Lydia Pettengill Taylor's recollections of childhood on the Kansas plains quickly changed from marvel to pain. She recounts her first memory of her parents. They were fighting, and her father was hitting her mother. They were shouting and violent with one another. Furniture and household items were broken in the fits of frenetic rage. Her father was an abusive man with an explosive temper. She vividly details how she

The Floating Brothel
of the Willamette

In the 1880s, the Willamette waterfront around present-day Portland was a tough section of real estate. The men didn't go to Sunday school. They liked their drinks hard, their women soft, and the law staying the hell out of their business. Local officials were corrupt, and each municipality was its own entity. Against this backdrop, an enterprising madam named Nancy Boggs did business. At this time, Portland was three cities: Portland, East Portland, and Albina. Each had different liquor laws and prostitution licensing. Nancy Boggs set up a floating whorehouse to avoid the local liquor taxes among the different opposing regulations.

Nancy had a sternwheeler that was forty feet wide and eighty feet long. To do business, she moored at a dock and took on customers. If she felt nervous about her location, she'd anchor in the river and run a small fleet of rowboats to take men to and from her establishment. The nature of her sinful business was not a threat to local municipalities. In fact, at least one chief of police had a healthy interest in a local saloon and was rumored to have invested in several dens of sin. What bothered the three municipalities had more to do with greed than morality. They didn't care about her corrupting local men or that she sold a lot of whiskey; they did care about the money she made and getting their share.

The sticky problem was that Nancy's floating saloon and bordello wasn't paying its fair share of taxes, fines, and bribes. Because she floated around and wasn't specifically connected to any town, she was getting by on a technicality, and this was not acceptable. Local law enforcement agencies

tried to raid her palace and force her to pay taxes on her lucrative trade, but she was too clever and managed to dodge all their attempts. Madam Boggs always seemed to slip away and be out in the river, a no-man's-land, before the police showed up. She had informants at the various city governments who tipped her about pending raids. Around 1882, several towns got together and tried a joint raid even though Nancy was moored out in the river. As the police approached, the ever-clever madam fought off the cops with hosed steam from the boiler room. She had prepared for such an event. The police returned to shore embarrassed but wiser. Nancy pulled anchor and moved her location. The police, now more determined than ever, took a more stealthy approach. In the dead of night with a mist on the river, a man quietly rowed out to Nancy's boat and cut the anchor ropes.

Spring runoff was at its peak and the current was stronger than usual. Caught by the current, the barge was starting to drift dangerously toward more open water. It seems either the boiler was not stoked—it took a fair amount of time to get it running—or there was a problem with the engine. Nancy told her girls not to worry. She got into a rowboat and made her way to shore as quickly as she could. As luck would have it, she ran into the captain of another sternwheeler. With her usual charm and promises only she could provide, Nancy convinced the good captain to rescue her boat. By the following morning, she was moored upriver and ready for business. When the captain sobered up is not known.

The brush with disaster persuaded Madam Boggs that the times were changing. She sold her boat and set up a bar and brothel on shore. She paid her taxes and was welcomed at last as a valued landlubber in the community of sin.

In the early years, businesses that plied the Portland waterfront could take advantage of vague jurisdictional boundaries and lax law enforcement.
COURTESY LIBRARY OF CONGRESS.

saw him with both hands around her mother's neck, choking and throttling her. Afterward, he punched her with closed fists. Lydia and her siblings were so frightened by the display that they ran and hid in the fields and the barn until her father's anger faded lest they were next to taste his fury. On another occasion when her father was angry, he kicked Lydia down the stairs, knocking her out.

Before farming in Kansas, the family had lived in Jacksonville, Florida, where her father was unsuccessful in business. They had lost almost everything, so they relocated to a farm five miles from Beloit, Kansas, in the north-central part of the state. They lived in a dugout "soddy"-style dwelling built into a hill with a poorly framed shack on the front. The house was cold and drafty in winter and dusty and hot during summer. During a rainstorm or a snow melt, the shack leaked. Except in the cold months, wandering snakes—including rattlers—and rodents were common. Bugs and spiders were an everyday occurrence. Their furniture was inexpensive or homemade. The floors were hard-packed dirt. It was a hand-to-mouth existence where both mother and father worked from before first light until after dark. The children were expected to help.

Lydia was easily sunburned. She had light blue eyes, taffy-colored hair, and long braids. Lydia remembers being told by both her father and her mother that she was too stupid to learn anything in school. She loved tending the cattle because she was out of the house and could feel the freedom of the open plains. Her mother had a sour disposition and was not given to kind remarks. Lydia's job was to tend to the livestock, specifically the family cattle, while they grazed on the prairie. She resented being told that she was stupid because she knew she had a keen imagination, and she liked to learn. She dreamed of a better life beyond the prairie.

Lydia wondered why Santa only came to good children or children with wealthy parents. In the evening she would sneak out of the house and look at the stars drifting across the sky. She wondered about the vastness of nature. She had to be careful and not let her mind drift too much. If an animal wandered off or got away, she was harshly "punished and sent to bed without supper," or worse.

Her father had a wanderlust and was never satisfied with his current status. As a former forty-niner, he never ceased looking for that big strike that would make his fortune. He constantly searched for the proverbial pot at the end of the rainbow, but never found it. As a result, he never stayed in one place long enough to be successful. The family could not make a success out of the farm, so her father decided to move. He blamed the bad land for their failure. The move from northern Kansas was especially traumatic for young Lydia and was, therefore, memorable. She had a dog she loved, and her father refused to let him come with the family. Lydia begged her father to let her take the pet, but he'd made up his mind. They would tie the dog up when they left so it couldn't follow the wagon. She comments that he had a "wicked, vile" temper. She also notes that animals acted on instinct, but humans, like her father, were vile by nature. Before the family moved, young Lydia would slip into the barn with her dog. She would check to make sure her father wasn't nearby. She dare not inflame his temper. Then she'd shout and scream and curse at him for making her leave her beloved pet. Because both her mother and father had foul mouths, she remembers that her cursing vocabulary was extensive even at an early age.

Her father moved the family to near Wichita. He rented twenty acres of good land and went into the hotel business while he farmed. He wasn't successful at either venture, so he left the family to pursue a business opportunity in Alabama. By this time they were quite destitute. Her father scraped up enough money for two months' rent before he left, but there was only a little food left in the kitchen. All the family had to eat was a sack of grits and a few jugs of molasses. Her mother and the children needed to fend for themselves, and many nights they went to bed hungry.

During one particularly bad stretch of luck, the family was close to starving. Lydia's wealthy aunt (her father's sister) invited them to come to Minnesota until they got on their financial feet. Her uncle offered her father a good job. The family was given a place to stay with all the extras. Lydia comments that her cousins were snobbish about the ragged condition of their poor cousins' clothing. "I keenly felt my own shabbiness and my inferiority, and this shabbiness made me appear more out of place than I would have felt had I been dressed with some degree of taste. . . . Their greatest delight was in teasing me about my ugly dress." In spite of their financial reversal, Lydia's mother was not sympathetic toward her daughters, nor did she understand how much the spousal fighting upset her children. Lydia enjoyed the schooling her family's new prosperity afforded, but she was not an outstanding scholar. After three years of formal education, it came as a shock when her mother told her that school was wasted upon her because she was stupid. Instead of getting an education, she was sent to a dressmaker for an informal apprenticeship.

Her parents continued to fight. It was at this time that she learned from her cousins that her parents were not legally married and that her mother had run away with her father. He had been previously married and had abandoned his former wife and children for her mother. Lydia's parents had six children together, but the union was less than congenial.

Wanting to escape her situation, at age seventeen Lydia reluctantly decided to marry a twenty-year-old bookkeeper. Her mother "rushed" the marriage, telling her that if she didn't join him at the altar, she would be kicked out of the home anyway because she wasn't wanted. Her new husband turned out to be a lazy provider who worked a total of two weeks in two years. Lydia supported them with her needlework. Frustrated and fed up with her husband, Lydia ran away and headed to Butte, Montana. She tried to find sewing work, but times were hard. She took a job as a chambermaid. Later she met a man with whom she developed a close relationship. She said he made her happy and bought her books. The two talked. For the first time, she writes, she'd met a man who treated her nicely. "I learned through a man I was living with that which I should have been taught years before in my home life." He bought her dresses, jewelry, and nice hats. He died suddenly and unexpectedly, and it broke her heart.

When she was twenty years old, she moved in with her sister. Both were destitute, and work was scarce. Lydia says, "[We were] just two more girls hungry and destitute, seeking for food and shelter, and despite our vaunted Christian civilization, having to go to hell to get them." When their situation became desperate, she writes, "Just two more victims to pander to the vice of man. Man . . . the protector of women, but always the destroyer of them." To keep from starving and to have a shelter to live in, she continues, "The house where we went was large, richly and elaborately furnished . . . [in] perfect taste and skill . . . every thing had been done for the sole

This Wyoming brothel was not unlike many Lydia worked at during her career. There would be a madam, a piano player/bouncer/bartender (called the professor), and a handful of girls. COURTESY HISTORY COLORADO, FRED MAZZULLA COLLECTION.

object of lulling the mind away from care and into a dream of forgetfulness." The life that she was forced into offended her senses and her sensibilities. "People who have always had plenty to eat," she writes, "little realize how good food tastes to those who have had to go hungry for a good while." She and her sister traveled and worked together in the oldest profession, but they eventually went in separate directions. The bawdy lifestyle had affected them both, and they drew apart. Her sister lost weight and was down to ninety-three pounds. She was likely addicted to laudanum, or some other opiate. The two parted ways in Cheyenne, Wyoming. Lydia sadly writes, "She passed out of my life."

Men would pay for her body, and she could eat on a regular basis if they did. In a guilty despair, she pens, "The wind had blown the good fates to one side, and the victims of vice had two more souls added to their number on that day." Lydia tried to get out of her profession a number of times but without success. She periodically tried to make her way as a seamstress, especially after she found a man to live with or marry. On several occasions, she worked with traveling theatrical troupes, but she seemed to find her way back to prostitution when times got hard.

Most prostitutes were always on the move, going to different states and towns. Lydia followed this pattern, visiting many places in her line of work. She moved from state to state and town to town—from Mexico to Canada. She enjoyed the travel, but the work numbed her. "I had schooled myself, not to care—not to think." While she was employed, she could not have company call upon her in her house, but would have to meet the person at a prearranged spot. There was little about the life that lent itself to making any kind of friend.

In Anaconda, Montana, she married again. It was a poor match. She took up dressmaking in a small-roomed apartment, using a curtain to divide the space. Her husband was a saloon keeper who quickly neglected her. Many nights he didn't come home, and he often cheated on her. She says she should have known better since she had known how saloon keepers lived when she was a prostitute. She divorced him. Lydia was a keen observer of life but a poor judge of men. Anxious to escape the world of prostitution, she married other times and lived with men—all with disastrous results. Several of the men she was involved with took financial advantage of her, and besides taking her money, property, and jewels, left her in debt.

Lydia was a solitary individual. She didn't enjoy the company of the women she worked with, and she had a poor opinion of the men who associated with her professionally. She was at odds with her conscience and never gave up hope of finding a better life. She writes, "I have gone to my lonely room, after a hard, nerve-racking night of boisterous song, laughter and drunkenness, and, oh, so often have I turned out the light and gazed out upon and across the city . . . [I would] throw off my mask, and ask God, Who knows all, to forgive a frail, weak-minded, erring woman her sins."

In diatribes she beats herself up and chastises herself. Then she lashes out at men who visit prostitutes. She argues that man is not woman's best friend. Rather he is "our worst enemy. He flatters our vanity and . . . we are foolish enough to listen to his praises and silly platitudes." A man will lead women on to fall to the same level as he. A man will often help a woman, but usually with an ulterior motive. "All men, no matter how base and corrupt they are, admire purity and goodness." A man will tire of a woman he can manipulate. "Remember, 'virtue is its own reward.'" She continues to say that those in the underworld of prostitution understand how dress affects men and how such women "use this to draw and ensnare the brainless kind, and they are disgustingly easy."

She ends her history by saying, "May kind blessings be on all who are sincere and live a good clean life, and may God help all to see the folly of wickedness." Lydia leaves us with the hope that she could be a crusader for women and families. Her dream was to lecture on women's rights or on the folly of prostitution and the pettiness of both men and women who are engaged in this damaging act. In the meanwhile, she hoped to change her profession and travel abroad. Her other goal was to learn French. Like most women in her profession, even after the publication of her book, Lydia drifted out of history and into obscurity. ✂

CHAPTER FOUR

POLLY BEMIS
The Chinese Poker Bride

I n 1862, James Warren discovered gold in what would soon become
Idaho Territory. By 1863, the boomtown known as Warren or Warren's
Camp had swelled to over 2,000. With it came the vices a prospector
with gold in his pocket expected. The search for gold was a high-stakes
gamble, and the outcome could be fortune or ruin. Life in Warren's
Camp could also be a gamble, except that fate rested on a roll of the dice
or the turn of a card. According to Old West lore, one of the most famous
poker games in history took place in this boomtown.

A man named Hong King, as the story is recounted, owned a saloon,
a dance hall, and a whorehouse. One night he was playing a wicked
game of cards with a hotshot gambler named Charlie Bemis. It was high-
stakes poker, no holds barred. Hong King started off with several good
hands, but as the evening wore on, Lady Luck frowned on him, and the
cards would not play in his favor. Charlie was a tough man and handy
with a six-gun, but he was known throughout the gold fields as an honest poker player, and King knew it. The night wore on as each man
drank and smoked and played. Charlie won some good hands and was

sitting pretty. His face was expressionless. An inveterate gambler, Hong King knew that a couple of hands in his favor would even things up. He knew bad luck could turn to good luck as quickly as a young girl's wink. Always the optimist, he took a stiff shot of red-eye, quickly looked at his cards, and set them down. This was the hand that he'd been hoping for. He went for broke. Hong King was out of money, but he had one last trick. She was a very pretty Chinese slave girl. Her name was Polly, and she was not only a popular girl in his brothel, but she had been his personal concubine. He'd paid good money for Polly, and she'd been worth every penny. Men came from miles around and paid plenty of gold for a whirl with this Chinese beauty. Hong King estimated that she was worth about $3,000. He'd drawn a good hand and was sure he'd win, so he staked Polly. Charlie knew Polly and was quick to take King's marker. There was nothing else left. King was sure he had won. Charlie showed his cards and for the first time smiled. He had pulled the better hand.

The clever gambler took King's cash, some property, and his Chinese slave. From then on, Polly became known as the Poker Bride of Warren, Idaho, or the Poker Bride. Charlie smiled. It had been a very good evening, indeed. He loved to gamble. But what should he do? He could keep Polly for himself—or maybe lease her to a brothel or a dance hall. She was a pretty girl, so he decided to keep her.

Or so the tale is told. Fact or fiction?

We're not exactly sure how Polly came to be with Charlie Bemis because this part of her history is obscured by a very good story. We know more about Polly than we do about most working women in the West and certainly more than we know about most Chinese women. Sadly, their stories are mostly unrecorded. Still, there are gaps to be filled, even with Polly, especially about her early life in China and her being smuggled into San Francisco, then Portland, and subsequently to the Idaho gold fields. Later in her life, Polly gave several interviews to Eleanor Gizycka in 1922. She also did other interviews before her death (some when she was eighty), and the *Sunday Oregonian* newspaper ran a lengthy piece about Polly on November 5, 1933, the day before she passed away at the hospital in Grangeville, Idaho. Polly's close friends also spoke about her life. Most of the information we have gleaned about this interesting woman occurs after her marriage to Charlie Bemis on August 13, 1894. Still, some parts of her life are obscured by time and myth, and the real account of how she came to be with Charlie is still out of focus. Regrettably, we don't know more. The details of her early life as a young woman who was sold to bandits in China, and her other adventures, would be fascinating. It would also be interesting to know more about her life in Warren before Charlie Bemis. We don't know when the poker game actually happened or, for that matter, if it happened. But it made a good addition to frontier mythology. As a point of fact, Hong King doesn't show up in the local census, nor are there records of him having a business license for a saloon. Charlie was reported to be a saloon owner in some histories, but we have no other records of his business. A breach in the historical records isn't mutually exclusive. We know from other sources that Charlie lived in the area. We also have to remember that there was a pronounced racial divide, and records of Chinese businesses might have been carelessly documented, or not documented at all. At the time, several other Chinese men were in Warren who might have had the funds to buy Polly. One of these men might have gone by a name approximating Hong King. And most telling, what were the odds that a respected Caucasian like Charlie Bemis played high-stakes poker with a Chinese gambler in a public saloon? For that matter, what were the odds of a white man like Charlie marrying a former Chinese slave and prostitute? In the nineteenth century, most white Westerners looked down upon Celestials, as Chinese immigrants were known, much as white Southerners looked down upon African Americans. Prejudice against Asians was extreme.

Many Chinese immigrants seeking economic prosperity came to the California gold rush in the early 1850s. It wasn't long after this that "Chinese Go Home" could be heard in gold camps. The unemployed and hard-on-their-luck were especially angered and blamed the Asians for their situations. Less than a decade later, when the gold was playing out in California, open hostility broke out as Chinese workers competed for jobs and moved on to other strikes. Exacerbating this racial anger, a large number of Chinese workmen were employed to help build the Central Pacific Railroad. Soon, local exclusionary laws were passed against the Chinese, and physical violence was unfortunately all too frequent. The Page Act in 1875 and the Chinese Exclusion Act in 1882 specifically outlawed Chinese immigration with few exceptions and denied citizenship to all Chinese. In 1892, the Geary Act renewed the Exclusion Act and required every Chinese in the United States to have a certificate of residence to prove he or she had entered the country legally. This document had to be carried on the person at all times. Failure to have it meant a year of hard labor or deportation or both. Furthermore, no Chinese were allowed to give testimony in court, nor was bail granted in habeas corpus cases.

How Polly was freed from her slavery is still a mystery. We can't entirely discount the story of the poker game, but the lack of details makes it hard to verify. If the famous poker game occurred, it had to have taken place sometime between the mid-1870s and 1880, since Polly shows up with Bemis on an 1880 census. Polly denied the poker game in her reminiscences, but, as mentioned, she was intentionally vague on some areas of her past because of the laws of the time. She could also have been trying to preserve her and Charlie's dignity since she didn't like being labeled as a poker bride. It's unlikely we'll ever know for sure. It's not something she talked about. Interestingly, as a new generation moved into Warren's Camp, several of her friends were completely unaware of the Poker Bride story. Otis Morris, whose stepfather knew Charlie Bemis, commented that the Poker Game Bride legend started with a man named Jay Czizek. Other historians, however, such as Sister M. Alfreda Elsensohn, argued that Charlie probably did win Polly in a card game. An early Warren resident named Taylor Smith claims that he and a handful of other men actually watched the card game. Given the prejudice of the times, we are, today, naturally more curious than someone of her day. The poker game provides a handy reason for the connection; besides, it makes a great story since high-stakes poker games were an important part of Western history.

The story of Polly Bemis, slave, prostitute, concubine, dance hall girl, laundress, wife, pioneer, is the tale of a life well lived. It's a story of racial intolerance, courage, and hope. Until Polly was in her late thirties, we simply have to piece her story together the best we can, knowing that we are combining our best educated speculation with legend and fact.

In 1922, Polly agreed to sit for an interview with Eleanor Gizycka (nee Eleanor Patterson). Gizycka's father was publisher of the *Chicago Tribune*, her brother was publisher of the *New York Daily News,* and Gizycka herself ended up owning and running the *Washington Herald* and *Washington Times* (eventually merging as the *Times-Herald*). In the interview, Polly said she was born on September 11, 1853. Of course her real name was not Polly (Polly was a slang term for a Chinese girl). Her real name was LaLu Nathoy. Her parents were poor farmers, and their precarious situation was further compromised by a severe drought that struck northern China. To save the family, her father sold his daughter so he could buy food for his family and seed to plant in his fields. This practice, which seems barbaric to us, was not uncommon in a culture that placed little value on female children. Most of the Chinese girls and women who came to the United States in the nineteenth century were sold by their families to slave traders for the express purpose of prostitution.

Some evidence suggests that Polly may not have been Chinese at all, but Mongolian. This might help explain her spunky behavior (uncharacteristic of most Chinese women in that culture and century) and why she took so readily to living in the wilderness. The Daur Mongolian tribes that had moved into northern China before Polly's birth had not yet abandoned hunting or their outdoor traditions. In most other ways, they assimilated into the Chinese culture. As was the custom, boys were preferred over girls in Chinese families. A girl was considered a liability, while boys were expected to take care of their parents in old age. When Polly was eighteen years old, she was sold to bandits or a broker who brought her, with other girls, to Shanghai. She survived the journey across the Pacific in a Chinese slave ship. The women, many of whom were only ten to fifteen years old, were packed into the holds of these ships like kippers. They were poorly fed, and sanitary conditions were abysmal. Disease and death were common. The sailors and officers were encouraged to "condition" the cargo since most would become prostitutes. They were repeatedly raped. Any spirit or dignity they possessed was stripped from them, so they'd be ready for their new life.

Legend has it that Polly was smuggled into San Francisco in a padded case to get past customs. She was then purchased for $2,500 and sent to Portland, Oregon, probably by pack train but possibly by ship. From Oregon she was transported to the Idaho gold fields. Sold into prostitution, she was lucky to have escaped the crib houses in the big city. There a girl lived in a room about the size of a bathroom in a modern tract home. The windows were barred as well as the doors. In these conditions a girl would live and die in her room since most women were never permitted to leave.

Polly's apparent fate, however, was to be a concubine or a prostitute in a brothel. On the pack trip from Oregon to Idaho, she probably dressed as a boy or man to mask her gender, so she could travel more easily. At least in a western town such as Warren, she'd have more freedom than she'd have in a large city. Still Polly was virtually a slave, an illegal alien with no civil rights in a country that didn't want or care about her. She was also enslaved by Chinese tradition that had guided her family for generations. To fight against her circumstances would bring disgrace to her family. Or worse, girls were told that if they ran away or refused to cooperate, their families in China would be killed.

If the legend about the poker game is fact, the price paid for Polly would be in line with the current market values for a good-looking Chinese woman in the West. If the game occurred, we can see how expensive King's poker game would have been. Pretty girls were difficult to procure. Losing Polly would be costly.

Chinese men would certainly be allowed to visit a Chinese prostitute, but it was socially unacceptable for a Chinese man to visit a woman from a white brothel. In fact, it could be a capital offense enforced by mob rule. A Chinese man could count himself lucky if he got only a solid beating for visiting a white woman. Chinese bawdy girls, in spite of the prejudice, fascinated white men, who found them strangely mysterious. In Idaho gold country, Chinese men were allowed to work in the food or laundry trades but were not allowed to mine without a license. In Idaho, a Chinese miner was taxed $4 a month, but he was only permitted to work claims that had been abandoned. However, before a permit was granted, the townspeople would have to vote first to see if an Asian man would be allowed to mine in the area at all. There was no tax for a white miner.

Polly arrived in Idaho in the 1870s. We're pretty sure that she knew Charlie in some capacity from the time she arrived. Perhaps he had visited her professionally. If Idaho lore is correct, the two had been friends for some time before the alleged poker game. Apparently, Charlie wasn't bothered by the prejudice, or he wanted the companionship of a woman, no matter what her ethnicity. In that day, the Chinese were considered inferior (Chinese men much more so than women). Chinese women didn't draw as much racial bigotry largely because women didn't compete with white men for jobs. Also, a lonely man in a boomtown with few women about couldn't be too choosy. In the West, Chinese women were mocked and stereotyped, but they still drew a man's attention. Old West legend says that Charlie Bemis met the young Chinese girl the first day she arrived in Warren. Someone was supposed to have said, "Here's Polly," and the stereotyped nickname stuck.

Polly was congenial and well liked. Later on, she was good friends with her neighbors on the Salmon. This was unusual in a culture that viewed Asians, at best, as second-class citizens. Polly was known as a generous and affable woman to those who knew her. When some of Polly's friends in later life reflected on her life, many discussed the high points but conveniently skipped over her life as a prostitute, how she came to be with Charlie, or her life as a slave. Polly had a number of white friends who enjoyed her company, which was unusual. One reason might have been that Polly was able to adapt to her new country, unlike so many of her countrymen. She didn't cling to the traditions of the old country or have any apparent ties to China. She probably converted to Christianity and was able to speak English effectively. She cooked and ate American food and wore American clothing. Polly could use a rifle and bagged game for the cooking pot, something few Chinese women, or men for that matter, could do. She embraced her new country wholeheartedly and loved living in America and especially being free.

She was an attractive woman, but she was chattel until she married. In Warren, she was worth about $3,000. The purpose of her life was not self-fulfillment, but service. She was a money-making tool, just one more woman to be bought and paid for. Hong King, or some other flesh broker, had taken her into his own home for his own pleasure. But mostly he was a businessman, and Polly was good business.

Prostitution was not her fault; it was her fate. Polly was fortunate that she escaped and found some measure of happiness with Charlie. But we can't lose sight of why she was in Warren: the sex trade. She was too

Crossing Racial Barriers: A White Man's World

Prostitution itself was not a racially isolated practice. However, if a Caucasian woman was arrested for prostitution, there would be no mention of race. If a non-Caucasian woman was arrested, her race was generally a factor, frequently as a racial slur. In print, she might be referred to as a Nig, a Coon, a Greaser, a Jap, a Minnie Jap, a China, a Polly, or a Celestial. Barroom gossip was likely even uglier.

There was another unwritten rule, too, a double standard, that if broken was usually enforced with a vengeance. A white man could go to a brothel of white, brown, yellow, or any other color of women without prejudice. But if a non-Caucasian man visited a white brothel or prostitute, he was generally in serious trouble if he was caught. In one town, a desperate woman was arrested for doing business with a black man. Normally, the local fine for running a disorderly house was $1, $5, $10, or $15, depending on the judge's mood. This woman was sentenced to three months in lockup plus a fine. The man in question was also locked up for three months—and many thought he got off easy. The judge wanted to set an example. In some parts of the West, the John might also have been beaten up or lynched. Crossing racial barriers was a serious offense—unless you were white.

The social hierarchy among prostitutes was Caucasian (French women commanded the highest prices), followed by Latin women. In last place were Blacks, Chinese, Japanese, and Indians.

valuable for anything else. Some have wondered, since she doesn't show up in early historical documentation, if she really was a prostitute. We'd like to think she escaped this horror, but such an assumption would be Pollyannaish. If we look at the circumstances, the flesh trade is the only logical conclusion we can draw. A teenage girl from China isn't smuggled into a California port under dangerous circumstances, sold, transported to Portland, perhaps sold again—then packed off to the Idaho gold fields to do laundry or boil rice. Polly was sold for a great deal of money in China and again at the flesh auction in San Francisco. Furthermore, it also cost a great deal of money to transport her several thousand miles to the gold fields. Why would anyone invest so much money in her? She could make someone a small fortune. Prostitution was the only profession that would yield a return on such an investment. Think of it another way. In an average western town, it would take the typical wage earner more than ten years to earn as much as Polly cost—that's if he put every penny he earned into the bank. She was an expensive piece of merchandise. Also, we have to consider what George Bancroft said. He was a close friend of Polly's. "[She] got money from women's time-honored methods."

As we've learned, Charlie and Polly were not only friends before they became associated, but they had some sort of a relationship, perhaps even a love interest. There's speculation that Charlie was her customer, but that the business transaction grew into a friendship and probably into genuine affection. Then there was the card game or some other incident that freed her from Hong King (or whomever). Around this time Polly gave up or was allowed to give up her venal life for other tasks. It is commonly thought in some circles that she might have been a madam or managed a house of bawdy Chinese girls under Charlie's direction, but there is no evidence of this. The good news is that, once she was with Charlie, she was no longer a slave and appears to have earned or been granted her freedom.

In 1890, Charlie, the inveterate gambler, found himself in a poker game with the wrong man. He was a bad-tempered card slick named John Cox. He proved to be a sore loser. The day after the game he came back and insisted that Charlie give him $250, or he'd shoot Charlie in the head. Charlie Bemis was a tough man and a good shot, but the abruptness and sheer cheek of the bad loser must have taken him by surprise. But after a lifetime of reading card players, he probably noticed that this fellow wasn't completely sane. Perhaps Charlie thought they could talk out their differences, or he was surprised by such bravado. Gambling in the West was taken seriously, and a gambling debt was considered a debt of honor. Coming back the next day and asking for your poke was dishonorable, especially with someone like Charlie, who was noted for being an honest player.

We don't know if Charlie laughed in Cox's face or said no. Cox pulled out his .45 and fired, blasting Bemis in the cheek and shattering bone. It was a serious wound, and Charlie came close to being fitted for a set of angel wings. When the bullet hit Charlie's face, it fragmented, along with pieces of his cheekbone. The doctor from Grangeville was summoned, and he recovered as many pieces of the ball as he could, as well as a half dozen pieces of bone. After a half hour of surgery, he knew there were more fragments, but he was afraid to dig any further. His biggest fear was infection. He said that the rest would be up to the man's immune system, but that Charlie had a chance. Polly stayed by Charlie's side for a month, cleaning his wounds and applying Chinese medicine and changing the bandages. Several times Polly removed more fragments with her crochet hook. She also found more lead, which she removed. Charlie credited her with saving his life, and he never forgot it.

The two evidently lived together after Polly nursed Charlie. There appears to have been a deep friendship if not a love between them. With the Geary Act of 1892, Polly's status in the United States was shaky. She could not prove that she was in the country legally, and both she and Charlie feared that she might be deported. They married in 1894. This doesn't sound out of the ordinary today, but in the 1890s this was a revolutionary, if not a shocking, course of action. You had sex with Chinese women, but if you were a white man, you sure as hell did not marry one. Tongues must have wagged.

Their friends, who were as racially open-minded as Charlie, witnessed the nuptials and cheered the two on. Wanting a little more privacy, and maybe wanting to avoid local gossip, the couple moved to a homestead about twenty miles from Warren on the Salmon River. The canyons on either side of their homestead formed steep walls. They had a large garden where Polly grew produce for Charlie to sell in Warren when he went into town to gamble or check on his business interests. They also grew berries and fruit. Polly would occasionally go to town, but she loved her home nestled in the steep canyon. She raised poultry and fowl. Charlie loved the homestead, but he realized he wasn't much of a farmer. He enjoyed relaxing and watching his wife in her garden, or watching her at one of her favorite pastimes—catching fish in the Salmon. In 1896, after navigating a great deal of red tape, Charlie got Polly a certificate of residence.

Polly Bemis wore her best dress on her wedding day in 1894. It was very unusual for a white man to marry a Chinese woman. Polly would be around forty when this photo was taken.

Charlie and Polly Bemis eked out a rustic but pleasant life along the Salmon River near Warren, Idaho. COURTESY IDAHO STATE HISTORICAL SOCIETY, 62-44.5.

In 1922, Charlie was suffering from health problems. Tragically, in August the cabin caught fire. Polly and a neighbor were able to get Charlie out, but he'd taken in a lot of smoke, and his health worsened. He died at 3 a.m. on October 29 and was buried the same day at the Shepp ranch where they were staying. A new cabin was planned. Polly lived in Warren for a couple of years while her cabin was being rebuilt. Her friends built and paid for her cabin with the condition that they'd get the land when she died. Charlie had only applied for a mining claim and not a homestead. Being Chinese, Polly could not inherit the claim or the homestead because she did not have citizenship. Her friends, Charlie Shepp and Pete Klinkhammer, stepped in to help her. Shepp acquired the mining claim so that he could protect her home. She moved back into her rebuilt home in 1924.

Her neighbors across the river had a phone line stretched across so they could check on her. By the early 1930s she was getting frail. In August 1933, she failed to call and check in. Her friends rowed across the Salmon to check on her. She was quite ill. They took her out of the canyon on horseback and got her to the hospital at Grangeville. Later she was moved to a nursing home. She missed her cabin but was cheerful and had many friends come visit. She grew more ill, and on November 6, 1933, Polly Bemis joined her ancestors. In 1987, her body was reburied near her home on the Salmon River. Her cabin is now a museum and on the National Register of Historic Places. ⚊

CHAPTER FIVE

HATTIE LAPIERRE

She Put a Few Slugs into the Man Who Forced Her into Prostitution

In Thermopolis, Wyoming, a bad case named Harry H. Black (his real name was Frank McKinney) was passing time in the Bar and Woods Saloon. Harry considered himself a bad man. He bragged about fleeing from the Royal Mounted Police in Canada after a couple of killings. It was rumored that he'd put lead in a couple of men in both New Mexico and Colorado. In Colorado, he'd been charged with murder, but there wasn't enough evidence to bind him over for trial. He liked to try his luck at the gaming tables, but he was a poor gambler, and he drank too much. He also used opium. Harry was a bully and picked on those he thought he could take. He was not above knocking a woman around, either, if she displeased him. In fact, he rather enjoyed it. A large, strong man, he generally paid for ladies by the hour, and he didn't care if he left bruises.

Hattie was a Southern girl, small-framed and pretty. For some reason, she fell for the sweet-talking Harry. At first, Harry showed Hattie a good time and was a perfect gentleman. She fell deeply in love. Harry promised they'd get married as soon as they moved to Lander, Wyoming. Excited about a new life and becoming a bride, Hattie quit her job and went with the man she loved. In Lander, they moved into a hotel as Mr. and Mrs. Harry Black.

The cards weren't turning right for Harry, but Hattie had not yet realized that she'd set her cap for the wrong man. Harry lost big in his gambling ventures and passed out markers. There were threats against his life if he didn't make good on his debts. It must have been quite a surprise to Hattie. It was as though the man she loved had turned into a different person before her eyes. Not telling her what he was doing or where he was going, Harry took Hattie to a local whorehouse and subcontracted her to the local madam. Hattie refused, of course, but for the first time, she saw the dark side of the man she thought she loved, emerging like a black shadow. She learned the hard way that Harry was not above physical abuse as he knocked her around for good measure. Furthermore, he threatened to kill her if she left the brothel. How could her life change for the worse so quickly? It was beyond her comprehension; she'd gone from preparing to be a bride to being a working whore. Harry told her that she was supporting their family by supporting him.

Hattie realized she had no choice. She knew Harry could easily kill her, or at the least, he was capable of hurting her badly. The shame of her condition and the repugnant acts she had to perform were physically sickening. Harry kept a close eye on her. He visited her often, not to give her words of comfort or appreciation or affection or thanks, but to take the money she had earned and threaten her with harm if she tried to run away. Ironically, although he'd brokered his fiancée for hire in a house of prostitution, he was insanely jealous if a patron paid too much attention to her. He'd threaten or fight any man who did more than simple business with Hattie. Few fought with him because he was a large man with an ill temper. After his frustration with other men was manifested, he'd take Hattie to her room and turn his rage on her. He'd punch her with his fists. One time he used the barrel of his gun on her head. Whatever love she had felt for Harry slowly turned to anger and hate.

Several times she tried to run away, but without success. Each attempt triggered more abuse from Harry. Even a whorehouse needs a certain amount of tranquility and solitude, so it was no surprise that Hattie was fired. The madam asked Harry to take Hattie and find another arrangement. Not only had Harry worn out his welcome at the local house, he'd worn out his welcome in Lander. Prudence dictated that he find a new town quickly. Harry's reputation as a tinhorn and his abuse of Hattie hadn't won many friends. In that day, few men would intervene in a "domestic" situation, but they looked down upon Harry for how he treated his wife. Men in the West hated to see a good horse whipped, a dog kicked, or a good woman beat up. It was a waste of good flesh.

The star-crossed pair headed back to Thermopolis where Harry hoped his luck would change. Much to Hattie's distaste, Harry made an arrangement with another madam and put Hattie to work in a place called the Stone House. Her embarrassment and disgrace were masked by her fear of Harry. It had been the longest six months of her life. Instead of being a bride and enjoying a long honeymoon with the man she loved, she was an inmate at a cathouse because the man she thought she loved needed her services. Hattie worried about getting pregnant and catching a disease. She'd been physically abused, pistol-whipped, raped, and forced into unspeakable acts by men she couldn't stand. Hattie was glad her family knew nothing about her plight. She had tried to hold back a little money so she could try another escape, but it was hard. Harry would beat her if he suspected. She would give in after he hit her. Her meager savings were gone.

She hated the shame she felt, especially when she was alone and she could cry. Her eyes were black and puffy from the last time Harry visited. He'd been in an especially vindictive mood. She thought that this time he might truly kill her. After he beat her, he took out his gun and told Hattie he was going to put a bullet in her. She'd be dead. To illustrate his intentions, he shot her in the foot. The slug ripped off part of her toe. When the law came to investigate, Harry told the officer that his weapon had accidentally discharged, and the whole thing was an accident. Hattie knew better. It was his way of warning her that if she didn't do as he said, the next time would be worse.

She thought about the pistol that she had in her luggage. Hattie had had enough and decided she would not be a whore, nor would she take this abuse any longer. She was also angry that Harry had bragged about being romantically involved with another woman. She knew her life was in danger, and it was obvious that the law wasn't going to do anything to help. Like all good stories, there are several versions of what was about to happen. You'll have to choose which one you like best. Both are eye-witness accounts. One was from the abused woman who refused to be a prostitute any longer and felt that Harry would kill her the next time he visited. The other story is from the dying Harry who claimed he was the wrongful victim of a mad woman's scorn.

Hattie's Version. Her toe hurt like hell, but Harry Black insisted that Hattie walk with him to his favorite saloon. He didn't want to make more of a scene at her place of employment. He didn't want her thrown out. When they were alone, he turned and threatened her again, telling her that he would kill her if she ran away or didn't cooperate. Hattie assumed that he was reaching for his gun to make the point. Fearing for her life and unwilling to take his abuse any longer, she pulled her own .38-caliber revolver and shot Harry. Shocked by what she had done, but not sorry, she ran as Harry stumbled to the saloon floor and collapsed.

Harry's Version. He was sitting in the saloon minding his own business having a drink when Hattie asked him to go for a walk. She asked for money, which he gave her. As he turned to go, she shot him in the back; he turned, and she plugged him near the chin. He stumbled back into the saloon and fell to the floor.

We know several things. They were walking together, and Hattie plugged Harry near the chin and put another one in his back. We also know that Harry somehow made it back to the saloon. We know that the doctor wasn't sure if he should remove the bullet. Harry talked a lot while he was wounded. It's also a fact that it took him four days to die.

Before Harry was properly dead and buried, Hattie was reported to have said, "She loved that man better than any man she ever saw," and something to the effect that she could not live without him. Whether this was a sincere confession or a clever strategy, we'll never know. The local law caught up with Hattie near midnight a week after the shooting and told her she was going to be taken to jail. However, the lawman, who had a soft spot for Hattie, told her he was hungry and took her to dinner, so she'd

Being confined to a jail cell was a shock for anyone, even those accustomed to life's hard knocks, as this unknown woman found out.

have a good meal under her belt. The law must have finally viewed her as a flight risk because she was then lodged in the local jail. After the hearing, her bail was set at $5,000. The prosecution argued that she purposely murdered Harry Black.

Hattie pleaded not guilty.

She went to trial in December, and the jury brought back a verdict of manslaughter and suggested that the court go light on her. They all knew how she'd been treated by Harry. The verdict was three years at the state prison. Many felt that Judge Carpenter's sentence was too harsh for her. Local support was in her favor. Hattie hired a new lawyer who started the appeals process. In one letter he sent to the Board of Pardons, he said he had collected more than 200 signatures, including the men on the jury. In the letter the signatories suggested, "Wherefore, your petitioners respectfully pray, the promises being considered that the Board of Pardons will recommend to his Excellency the exercise of his executive clemency and that he grant the said HATTIE LAPIERRE a pardon." The governor was happy to sign the document.

After a year and few months, Hattie walked out of the Wyoming State Penitentiary and out of history. She got on a train and was never heard from again. ⊷

Typical of penitentiaries at the time, the Wyoming State Penitentiary in Rawlins was a forbidding destination. COURTESY OF WYOMING STATE ARCHIVES, DEPARTMENT OF STATE PARKS AND CULTURAL RESOURCES.

They Called Them Hog Ranches

"I never saw a hog running about, but the girls were low and tough," a soldier commented. "Hog ranch" referred to the lowest rung of prostitution, U.S. Army whorehouses. Many have speculated on what the word *hog* means—likely it referred to the prostitutes, their living conditions, or the smells near their lodging. The word *ranch* probably relates to the location, because hog ranches were not in towns. They were rural dens of sin.

On some posts, a hog ranch had to be a certain distance from the post—often three to five miles. At other posts, ranches were near the enlisted men's quarters, frequently near their outhouses and the stables. During summer, the smell could be overwhelming.

Some hog ranch prostitutes were old and at the end of their sagging careers—there was no place else to work. Others were opium addicts or alcoholics. Some were ill (tuberculosis was common). Nearly all had venereal disease. Soldiers were among the lowest-paid men on the frontier—making less than cowboys. An enlisted man's working girl had to sell her services cheaply or starve, living well below poverty level. Because of their economic situation, living conditions were horrid. A woman at a hog ranch might set up shop in a tent, a dugout, a shack, or, if she was lucky, a small cabin. Some women worked alone; others might be overseen by a madam or a store manager. Servicing enlisted men on an army base was considered the lowest of the low. As one soldier said, "They were the ugliest women on the frontier." It was a standing joke that only "the army would take 'em' since no one else would." As one cowboy said, "A whore went to the dogs, then to the soldiers."

It was a hard life, and there was no recourse if a woman was the victim of physical abuse or rape. Alcohol and laudanum numbed the pain. Suicides, especially from overdoses and poison, were frequent. In 1877, Captain John G. Bourke, who had won the Medal of Honor during the Civil War, was stationed at Fort Laramie. He wrote in his diary about the prostitutes on a nearby ranch: "[They] were virgins whose lamps were always burning brightly in expectancy of the coming bridegroom, and who lured to destruction the soldiers of the garrison. In all my experience, I have never seen a lower more beastly set of women."

CHAPTER SIX

KITTY LEROY

Life and Death with a Finger on the Trigger

er legend was a tale of terror, lust, and murder. Kitty Leroy was larger than life and as unpredictable as the wild wind on the Northern Plains. A reporter wrote that "[Kitty] had five husbands, seven revolvers, a dozen Bowie knives and always went armed." At the least, Kitty was a prostitute, a dancer, a trick-shooter, and a gambler. She was also a successful madam.

The wind was blowing on a cold December night in Deadwood, South Dakota, in 1878. Samuel Curley had returned to town after a long absence. He had been gambling in Denver and Cheyenne—but mostly he was trying to forget Kitty. He couldn't get her off his mind. They had married in June 1877, but their relationship had turned toxic in a few months. If they had a common denominator, it was gambling, but apparently that was not enough to hold the two star-crossed lovers together. Kitty's affections had strayed to several men not long after the "I dos." But Samuel still loved her, and unless she came back to him . . .

Hanky panky was a risky business on the frontier, where men in particular were quick to take offense in matters of honor, and conflicts were often resolved by the squeeze of a trigger. COURTESY LIBRARY OF CONGRESS, 3A50185U.

he hated to think about what he might do. He loved her enough to kill her.

Sam had sent pointed messages to the men who were involved with his estranged wife. None had responded when he called them out. They were cowards. He wanted to show Kitty how much he loved her by fighting them. Ironically, it didn't bother him that Kitty was a working prostitute with bawdy girls in her employ. That was business, and he could accept that, if not respect it. It was part of her business. He didn't mind if she loved gambling. Sam could understand that. It happened that Kitty owned the successful Mint Gambling Saloon, which conveniently was the head-quarters for her brothel. What he hated was how much she flirted with other men in front of him, and her being with them. She'd had affairs be-fore they were married, but he hoped they'd stop once they tied the knot. Even worse, she may have lied to him. There was a chance they weren't re-ally married. He'd heard rumors that she had not been properly divorced from her last husband. In the Lone Star Saloon, depressed and desperate, Sam bragged that he might shoot his wife if she didn't come back. He scribbled a note to her to meet him in her rooms above the saloon.

Kitty received the note but didn't know if she should see Sam. He'd turned a little bit crazy. She knew what a temper he had and knew it had been a mistake to marry him. He was a second-rate card shark in his late thirties who had never made it big. He was a good gambler, but he was impatient, and he took shortcuts. Like her, he wasn't above pulling a card out of his sleeve if he could do it without being caught. She once thought she loved him, but she'd worked hard to get this far and wasn't going to share her saloon with a four flusher. Besides, she'd gotten bored with him. The only constant in her life was a card game, especially since she owned the gambling parlor, and the house had the advantage.

Kitty Leroy was nervous about what Sam had written in the note. For some reason, she'd made a will on December 6, 1878, shortly before their meeting. She always carried a pistol and a knife, and that comforted her. She could shoot an apple off a man's head while she was riding a horse. She'd made a living trick-shooting and could take care of herself. She de-cided to meet him, against her better judgment. But this would be the last time. She would never go back with him. This was a courtesy call for old time's sake, nothing else. Her life had never been better.

Sam ran up the stairs to the apartment above the Lone Star Saloon. He was too angry to notice the cold. He knew that Kitty had rented the place a week earlier. He knocked on the door—maybe a little too loudly, and she let him in. It was awkward. It was simple. He had a lot to say, but he couldn't articulate it the way he'd planned. It happened so fast. When she said, "No," Sam knew what he had to do, and he did it quickly. If he couldn't have her, no one could. Without thinking, he pulled the big revolver from its holster. He cocked the Colt, pointed it at the middle of her chest, and pulled the trigger. Sam watched in horror and amazement as the bullet lifted his unrequited lover off her feet. Kitty's expression changed to unbelief and then to serenity as her life leaked out of her. She sagged backward, as dead as a winter leaf. Sam barely noticed the bullet hole in her chest and the red spot that grew larger from the inside out. He didn't look at the diamond earrings she always wore. Kitty was the most beautiful woman he'd ever known. He loved her, damn it. Sam, almost numb, looked around and put the Colt to his forehead, thumbed back the hammer, and pulled the trigger. It had happened so fast.

The patrons from the Lone Star heard the shots and rushed upstairs, expecting the worst, and they found it. They discovered Leroy on her back with a bullet hole in her chest. Her brown wavy hair couched her face. Her eyes were closed, but she did not look peaceful. Samuel Curley was a damned mess. He'd fallen forward. Brains and gore and bits of skull were scattered about the room from the side of his head where the bullet had mushroomed as it exited. The murder-suicide was complete. He did not look peaceful, either.

And so the story was told and retold. No one is really sure what happened. What we do know is that on December 7, 1878, Kitty Leroy, prostitute, madam, saloon owner, dancer, trick-shooter, and gambler, was shot dead in her apartment. A few feet away, Samuel Curley, two-bit gambler, died of an apparent self-inflicted wound after he killed Kitty Leroy. The *Black Hills Daily Times* reported on the murder room:

> The bodies were dressed and lying side-by-side in the room of death. . . . A pretty picture of Kitty, taken when the bloom and vigor of youth gazed down upon the tenements of clay, as if to enable the visitor to contrast . . . . The pool of blood rested upon the floor; blood stains were upon the door and walls. . . . [the] cause of tragedy may be summed up in a few words.

We have to ask the question, who was this woman?

Like so many women of the West, especially bawdy women, there are fascinating fragments that can be pieced together, but they don't complete the picture. The facts and the legends are difficult to distill and separate. Kitty lived a troubled life at a time when being a disenfranchised woman was problematic. We're tempted to say that she had all the watermarks of a sexually abused child, but we don't know for sure. Nor were these kinds of things discussed in that time. It's tempting to further speculate, but there already has been a lot of conjecture. We can truthfully say Kitty Leroy's life was tragic and that she was a darned good-looking woman. She was flamboyant and extravagant, but how much of the frontier hyperbole was fostered by Kitty, who knew her audience loved a good show and grabbed all the headlines she could get? She never bothered to correct the stories told about her. The only thing that might have troubled her was if the stories were not being told. In her line of work, all publicity was good. This complicates the truth. She is shrouded in legend and bits of sensational journalism. Telling her complete story is like putting together a jigsaw puzzle with missing pieces, further complicated by handfuls of extra pieces from other puzzles.

While not always accurate, what we can piece together of her story is important and worth telling. At the heart of the legend, we sometimes find kernels of truth. Her birth date is uncertain, but an educated guess would be around 1850 in either Texas or Michigan. We know almost nothing of her early life except that legend has her dancing in public by the age of ten. By the time she was fourteen, she was dancing in saloons and dance halls. Kitty was reputed to be a talented dancer, and her reputation followed her to Deadwood. So did her status as a trick-shooter. At some point in her childhood, she put on dance shoes and picked up a rifle. We are not sure when she turned to prostitution to supplement her other activities. She's reported to have had five husbands, but no one is sure of the true number. She certainly lived with different men, but it's unlikely she was *legally* married five times. Her first marriage, reportedly, was at fifteen. In the nineteenth century, many girls were married at this age if not earlier. Texas legend has her shooting apples off her husband's head. The details are sketchy, but such trick-shooting could earn enough pocket change to eat and buy a bed on a good day. At some point, she added gambling to her résumé, and it became the constant in her life and her only true love. Faro and poker were her games of choice and her passion.

The Ghost of Kitty Leroy: May It Find Peace

Since Kitty Leroy and her murderer were buried in the same grave, the good folks of Deadwood felt the ghosts of both Kitty and Sam Curley may not have found rest. On February 28, 1878, the *Black Hills Daily Times* discussed their disembodied spirits in the following article:

> Kitty was a woman well known to the reporter, and whatever might have been her life here, it is not necessary to display her virtues or her vices, as we deal simply with information gleaned from hearsay and observation. With the above facts before the reader we simply give the following, as it appeared to us, and leave the reader to draw their own conclusions as to the phenomena witnessed by ourselves and many others. It is an oft repeated tale, but one which in this case is lent more than ordinary interest by the tragic events surrounding the actors.
>
> To tell our tale briefly and simply, is to repeat a story old and well known—the reappearance, in spirit form, of departed humanity. In this case it is the shadow of a woman, comely, if not beautiful, and always following her footsteps, the tread and form of the man who was the cause of their double death. In the still watches of the night the double phantoms are seen to tread the stairs where once they reclined in the flesh and lingered in loving embrace, finally melt[ing] away in the shadows of the night as peacefully as their bodies' souls seems to have done when the fatal bullets brought death and the grave to each.
>
> Whatever may have been the vices and the virtues of the ill starred and ill-mated couple, we trust their spirits may find a happier camping ground than the hills and gulches of the Black Hills, and that tho' infelicity reigned with them here happiness may blossom in the fairer climate.

The first real historical record we have of her comes from Dallas, Texas, in 1875. Kitty was a dancer and likely an occasional prostitute between dancing gigs. She performed at the Johnny Thompson Variety Theater where she was reported to have brought down the house. She also played cards. She was a beautiful woman and drew men into the venue like a magnet. Always looking for the next best hand, when a gambler talked about California and promised her a saloon and a gambling parlor of her own, she left her husband and headed west. When the man she ran off with couldn't deliver what he promised, she discarded him like a bad card and ran off with a more promising prospect. Frontier lore has her marrying for a second and a third time. If she actually married, it didn't turn out well for her third husband. They were having a big spat, so Kitty told her fiancé to go ahead and hit her. He responded in true cowboy fashion that he wouldn't hit a woman. Furious, she changed into men's clothes, came back, and said she had dressed like a man so he could hit her now. Her lover laughed aloud, so she threatened to shoot him. He told her to go ahead, but he wouldn't shoot back because she was a girl. In a blind rage, she pulled out her pistol, as the legend goes, and warned him one last time. He taunted her again, so this time she plugged him with her six-gun. She was afraid he was dying, so she told him they should get married right away. Kitty was always pragmatic. Then she called a doctor. The physician did the best he could, and the preacher stepped in and married them. Her new husband cleared her of wrongdoing, and Kitty was smart enough not to say a thing. They had a short honeymoon because her husband died several days later from the gunshot wound. Kitty moved on.

She had learned that she could make it on her own. Men were to be enjoyed or used, so you took what you could get and moved on when you reached diminishing returns. Stories about the gold country were more than this "widow" could take. Heeding the call, Kitty headed for Deadwood, where the action was. She's said to have ridden the stage into town with Wild Bill and Calamity Jane, but such a story is surely a tall tale. If you believe the legends, everyone of any note rode into Deadwood with either Wild Bill or Calamity. The truth is she did arrive in Deadwood. More important, the boomtown held just what she wanted. There was gold in the hills and gullible men to be fleeced, lonely men who wanted

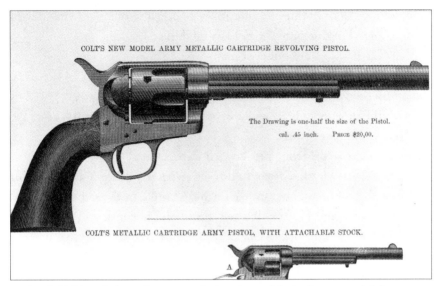

COLT'S NEW MODEL ARMY METALLIC CARTRIDGE REVOLVING PISTOL.

The Drawing is one-half the size of the Pistol.
cal. .45 inch.   PRICE $20,00.

COLT'S METALLIC CARTRIDGE ARMY PISTOL, WITH ATTACHABLE STOCK.

In the Wild West, Colt revolvers were the handgun of choice for personal defense as well as dastardly deeds. COURTESY LIBRARY OF CONGRESS, LC-US262-110403.

gambling and women. She also wanted a place of her own. Undoubtedly, she made her way by freelancing for a while, and when she had enough money, she opened the Mint Gambling Saloon, with a whorehouse upstairs. Some stories suggest she made enough to buy her new place. Others tell of her marrying a wealthy man who bankrolled her. Other legends tell how she rode a winning streak in a game of high-stakes poker . . . it's all a bit unclear. Some legends link her to a wealthy German prospector. If she married him, it didn't last long.

Regardless of how she procured the money, the Mint was a great success. Gambling, drinks, and women were a great way to separate men from their gold dust. In addition to the usual menu of vice and greed, Kitty favored the men by dancing for them, which was always a crowd-pleaser. She was also said to do some trick-shooting, which was always a big hit in any western town. She was known to be a careful woman, and one who went armed. Apparently she let her guard down the night Samuel came to meet her. She could easily have had a weapon in the folds of her dress or in a special pocket. Yet it appears Sam caught her flat-footed, which is surprising. How did he get the upper hand? She made a living out of reading men, but this time she made a fatal mistake.

Sam Curley would shoot a woman.

The *Black Hills Daily Times* in 1883 published this elegy in honor of the murdered woman: "Spirits of the good, the fair and beautiful, guard us through the dreamy hours. Kinder ones, but, perhaps less dutiful, keep the places that once were ours."

Ironically, the preacher preached a joint funeral to both Kitty's and Sam's plainly hewn pine boxes and their respective friends. To add insult to injury, the victim and her murderer were buried in the same grave. It is said, like Cathy and Heathcliff, their ghosts did not rest, and to this day, they haunt the Lone Star Saloon. Eventually, their remains were moved to unmarked graves in the Mount Moriah Cemetery in Deadwood. ⚔

CHAPTER SEVEN

ETTA PLACE

The Mystery Woman
of the Wild Bunch

tta Place was a mystery woman. We have her picture, so we know definitively that she was one of the most beautiful women in the American West—if not one of the most enigmatic. We know that Etta was the longtime companion of Harry Longabaugh, aka the Sundance Kid. We also know that Etta Place was a close friend of Butch Cassidy, the most successful outlaw in the West, and perhaps his one-time lover. The rest of what we know is speculation and hypothesis mingled with fact and circumstance. She is a very hard lady to pin down.

Was Etta a high-class parlor attraction at Fanny Porter's infamous house in Hell's Half Acre in San Antonio, Texas? Was she a school teacher? Could she have been a domestic at Fanny's brothel? What did Butch mean when he told a friend that Etta was an excellent housekeeper, but that she had the heart of a whore?

These questions and more have been asked by law enforcement, detective agencies, historians, and Wild Bunch buffs for more than a

The beautiful Etta Place and her lover, the Sundance Kid. In 1901, prior to leaving to South America, they posed for a photo. The watch on her lapel was purchased by Butch Cassidy at Tiffany's in New York.

COURTESY OF THE LIBRARY OF CONGRESS, IMAGE LC-USZ62-132506.

hundred years: Who was the real Etta Place? Where did she come from? What happened to her? And just as important, where did she go? To make matters interesting, around 1907 Etta quietly slips out of western history without a trace, leaving only speculation and wonder. The Pinkerton Agency was hired to run down the Wild Bunch. The Pinkerton detectives felt she was born around 1874, but more contemporary researchers speculate that she might have been born as late as 1879 or 1880. The Pinkerton agent who worked on her file made a typographic error transcribing her name as Etta (by which she has been known since). It should have been Ethel. We know even less about her true last name. "Place" was one of the names she took when she attached herself to Harry Longabaugh; it was his mother's maiden name. We know Etta stood about five feet, four inches tall, weighed 105 pounds, and had a dark complexion. She had rich, dark hair piled on her head, according to Marvel Lay, the daughter of Butch's best friend's wife. She carried herself with grace and style. Some of the Pinkertons felt she might have come from Texas because she could speak Spanish and knew how to cook Mexican dishes. Others speculate that she came from Utah, perhaps Joseph or Price, where she had lived with a Mormon family. Conjecture is that she might have first met Butch in Utah (not at a whorehouse in Texas). Others argue Etta was from the Midwest. We just don't know.

It seems likely that she was a sporting woman—and probably a parlor girl. A high-class boarder from Fanny Porter's, the Wild Bunch's favorite playground, appears to be a logical assumption. Unlike many madams, Fanny was fair with her employees and honest with her patrons. She also seemed to be a bit of a cupid. She wouldn't hold a girl in her service if she fell in love.

At the end of the Victorian period, when propriety was the order of the day, a proper girl would hardly go buggy riding without a chaperone after dark, let alone ride the Outlaw Trail with a bunch of known train robbers who were the most wanted men in the United States. Etta must have had a wild streak, a craving for adventure at her core. She took off across the country on the run, dodging marshals with two wanted men. And then, if that wasn't enough of an adventure for one woman, she sailed off to the frontiers of South America to start a new life—she was Wendy while

Butch Cassidy and the Sundance Kid were her outlaw Peter Pans. They never seemed to grow up.

While it was safe to assume that she was probably an expensive prostitute, she was reported to have good manners and was somewhat proper. However, she was not naïve. She was fully aware of what her two boys did at the office—robbing trains, banks, and payrolls—if they weren't rustling cattle or horses. Both had been in prison. They used cocked revolvers and threatened to shoot to kill if the money wasn't handed over. She must have noticed, though, that for wanted outlaws, both Sundance and Butch had a soft side for the small rancher and the little guy. Neither took pleasure in violence or the threat of violence. Rather, it was a tool, a stage act, to get what they wanted. They both understood it was one thing to rob, but the stakes were much higher if someone was killed. Butch was fond of saying that if you took their money, they'd chase you, but if you killed someone, a posse would come after you and not give up. Etta must have appreciated how both Sundance and Butch read constantly, especially Butch. He was a voracious reader. They were not like wild Harvey Logan, aka Kid Curry, their outlaw accomplice. Curry was a psychopathic killer who pulled the trigger without compunction, yet he treated prostitute Annie Rogers with kindness.

They were in the outlaw business, and violence, intimidation, and deadly weapons were an important part of their trade, and she knew it. While we have no evidence that Etta participated in any crime in the States, she was surely a working partner on their South American crime sprees. She knew how to use a firearm and was skilled on horseback. While she may not have participated directly in Wild Bunch crimes in the United States, at the least she was a criminal after the fact. She liked living the high life, and she liked the bundles of money the outlaws brought home so she could live the high life. She surely had fallen in love with Sundance before they left for New York, and they were apparently a committed couple, though their relationship may have begun as a business arrangement.

Etta may have been associated with Butch before she set her cap for Sundance. If this occurred, it likely took place in Utah. Or, Butch may have met Etta in a professional capacity before she began her long relationship with Harry Longabaugh, the Sundance Kid. We do know that Butch, Etta,

The Cheyenne Club catered to Wyoming's elite, the sort of social institution that might welocme a winsome belle such as Etta Place.
COURTESY AMERICAN HERITAGE CENTER, UNIVERSITY OF WYOMING.

and Sundance easily slipped through the nets that sooner or later managed to capture the rest of the Wild Bunch. The trio slid out of Texas and made their way to New York City where they had a luxurious vacation in the big city. Sundance and Etta must have been serious about each other. They traveled as man and wife, which was not so unusual. But when Sundance visited his family in Pennsylvania, he introduced her to his family and friends as his wife. Later we do know that the two lovers visited Dr. Pierce's Medical Institute. Sundance told his associates that he was being treated for an old leg wound, but some have speculated that one or both of the lovers were being treated for venereal disease (most historians agree that both Sundance and Butch had been bitten by "the go-to-town disease"). We know Sundance and Etta visited the Institute using assumed names. When detectives questioned the Pierce medical staff after the trio had sailed for South America, they were able to get a positive identification from photos. The outlaws' departure from the United States was well timed; thanks to the photographs taken in Fort Worth and New York, detectives were closing in.

The Star-Crossed Lovers: Annie Rogers and Kid Curry

Who would have imagined it? The stars must have crossed over Texas! A wild outlaw killer and the high-end parlor whore fell in love. The unlikely pair met at Fanny Porter's famous brothel in San Antonio. The outlaw happened to be Harvey Logan, aka the infamous Kid Curry, the same Kid Curry who was a personal friend of Butch and Sundance, the same Kid Curry who rode with the Wild Bunch. He was loyal to his friends, but if you crossed him, he would hunt you down and kill you.

In the late 1890s, Logan was the most wanted man in the country.

The gorgeous Annie must have seen qualities in Logan others overlooked. She said he was kind and considerate. Between lucrative jobs, the Wild Bunch took lengthy vacations, which gave Kid Curry time to go on long trips with his best girl. He bought her ice cream and took her on Ferris wheel rides. They enjoyed going East, pretending they were regular people, even husband and wife. Annie surely hoped the Kid would give up his outlaw ways and settle down, but she knew her man too well to push him.

Harvey Logan, aka Kid Curry, was a ruthless killer who nevertheless was a gentleman in his relations with prostitute Annie Rogers. COURTESY OF THE LIBRARY OF CONGRESS, IMAGE LC-USZ62-6131.

Their "arrangement" was the best she could expect. When Kid Curry joined up with the Wild Bunch for business, she went back to Fanny's. We know little about Annie's childhood or other relevant events. We do know, however, that she was very pretty, well educated, and carefully dressed. She worked for Fanny Porter and must have been good at her job. She also knew her Bible and quoted scriptures.

Rogers was amused by the Kid. On their trips, the Kid would wear silk underwear. They took long train rides (considering how much he enjoyed robbing trains, this is not surprising), had quiet suppers, and strolled about town. After Butch and Sundance left for South America, Curry pulled off a sloppy train robbery in the West and picked up Annie in Texas for another long vacation. (Curry was a bold outlaw, but he wasn't a master at planning jobs like Butch.) After some rest and relaxation, the pair of lovebirds was handily arrested in Nashville for passing stolen bills. Annie was implicated and jailed, but Curry did his best to clear her. She was eventually freed. Later, Curry broke out of prison and was shot and killed—at least we're pretty sure he was killed—after a robbery went sour. Annie went back to Texas, but we don't know where and if she continued her former line of work. Her secrets, unfortunately, disappeared with this fascinating woman.

New York was a great place to hide for a short time, but Butch was getting nervous and wondered if deputies or Pinkertons might be getting close (and they were). Sundance and Etta made a quick trip to see Niagara Falls and other sights on an informal honeymoon. Butch, to show his appreciation for Etta, bought her a lapel watch at Tiffany's. The couple, Etta wearing her new watch, also stepped into De Young's Photo Studios for a photograph. This would prove to be one of the few mistakes the wily outlaws would make. It would be as costly as the Fort Worth Five photo. It gave the army of detectives another name and a face, making a true escape more precarious. After a month-long vacation, the threesome sailed for Buenos Aires. Butch boarded the *SS Herminius*—Sundance and Etta may have sailed on another ship.

In South America they established a cattle ranch. Butch said the country looked like Wyoming, and he liked it. The outlaws went by the names of Santiago Ryan, Anna Marie, and Harry Place. A visitor to the trio's ranch commented that they had nice wallpaper, framed pictures, and lassos from horse hair on the wall. The observer also said that Etta was neatly groomed and comely. The expatriates established several successful ranches in different South American countries, but their pasts continued to haunt them. There was no extradition, but pressure from Pinkerton detectives at high government levels, along with other Pinkerton smear campaigns (blaming every robbery in the country on the outlaw gringos), started to have an effect. The three were tipped off by a police friend that there were warrants for their arrest. They packed their essentials and left.

We think Etta came back to the United States around 1903, perhaps for a vacation, maybe to see a doctor. Some have wondered if she was having a baby, an abortion, or seeking additional treatment for a venereal disease. Sundance probably came back with her. We know, however, that he was back in Argentina working on their ranch with Butch by 1904. Etta may have made other visits while she was in South America. There were sightings of Sundance and Etta in Texas during these years, but nothing that could be officially documented. Indeed, several of the so-called sightings occurred when we know Sundance was in South America. The reliability of the various reports is dubious at best.

By 1907, the lovely Etta Place left South America, never to return. We're reasonably certain she left by herself. She drifted into total obscurity. There is the usual speculation about where she went, but nothing is verified. Perhaps she died in childbirth in Denver, Dallas, or Fort Worth, or was crippled by venereal disease. Some speculate that she had a ruptured appendix and died under an assumed name in a Southern hospital. To add to the list of possible scenarios, she is rumored to have been a madam in Fort Worth or San Antonio. Maybe she took up school teaching. A logical but unproven scenario is that Sundance knew the detectives were starting to close in on the outlaws, and he wanted her safe. He sent her to the States with money, and she disappeared. Or, she might have fallen out of love. Perhaps she had grown weary of the outlaw trail and just wanted to live or raise her child (if she had one) in peace.

Being an intelligent woman, having dodged the law for years, she knew how to disappear, and she did. ⇥

CHAPTER EIGHT

EMILY WEST MORGAN
The Yellow Rose of Texas

R ight or wrong, Emily West was the woman behind the legend. In Texas mythology, right or wrong, she was the siren behind the song, *The Yellow Rose of Texas.*

As the story is told, the stunning Emily West was a sassy, beautiful mulatto woman who selflessly turned the tide in the war with Mexico. Before the Battle of San Jacinto, Santa Anna's troops swept across southern Texas like locusts. The Mexican president had boldly vowed to wipe out the republic's leadership once and for all. Overly confident and boasting a superior force, he split his army and pushed toward New Washington until he was almost close enough to spit. The Mexican soldiers could see the pickets and their enemy's campfires. Confident of victory, Santa Anna chose to postpone the attack because he needed a nap. He would engage the rebellious Sam Houston and his army later. His forces had taken the Alamo, so surely this scattered bunch of rebels would present no problem for his disciplined troops. During his rest period, the great Santa Anna was seduced by a curvy, long-legged mulatto who bought time for the struggling Texas patriots by taunting and

A notorious fashionista, Santa Anna was an easy target for the press, especially in defeat. COURTESY LIBRARY OF CONGRESS, LC-USZ62-62412.

teasing the lovesick general before she finally seduced him. In his large brown and white silken tent, the enchantress played waiting games with the president, using her feminine wiles, so he'd forget why he came—at least for a while. By sacrificing her virtue slowly, Emily bought the Texans enough time to rally and battle the superior foe.

Santa Anna liked women, and he liked his creature comforts, always traveling in style. In his opulent tent, he took his meals on exquisite china and ornate silver service. He drank the finest wines and liquors—only out of cut glasses. He also carried a large supply of opium, which he used liberally. He frequently indulged himself with the local women he captured or acquired. He called this pursuit the "gravy of society." At night or during the siesta, he liked to wear silken underwear. He moved his army across Texas invigorated by the harsh lessons he taught the rebels.

On this fateful day, the beautiful Emily, unlike most of his captives, seemed to like him. The afternoon tryst went much longer than usual. He noted that she looked almost Spanish with her beautiful yellow skin and long flowing hair. She toyed with him. While the female patriot courtesan and the opium-dulled general were playing parlor games in the tent under the oak trees, the Mexican army rested, rifles stacked by the cooking fires. Like their leader, they, too, were confident of an easy victory. While they rested, Texas soldiers crept into place. Many were less than thirty yards away in the tall prairie grass. When the battle cry was shouted, "Remember the Alamo," Texas bullets cut down the Mexican forces like a pigeon shoot. In less than twenty minutes, the battle was over. Over 600 Mexicans were killed, and more than 700 were taken prisoner. Incredulous, the slightly drunken, opium-addled Santa Anna stumbled out of his tent and grabbed the nearest horse. Something was wrong. Without dignity he galloped off in tailored silk undershorts. He was soon caught by the Texans. It was hard to miss a man in fancy silk drawers when all you'd ever worn was homespun.

Of course, everything is bigger in Texas, including the story of the Yellow Rose.

Sometimes it's better not to let a few facts get in the way of a damn good tale—especially if it promotes the glorious state of Texas. It didn't take long for the legend to become true, like George Washington and the cherry tree or Honest Abe being overpaid three cents. The Yellow Rose, Emily Morgan, quickly became an important part of Texan culture. Emily was, after all, one of the heroines of San Jacinto. She gave all for the cause of Texican freedom. The new republic was understandably proud of their victory, so a woman's virtue was a small price to pay for the lives she saved and for the defeat of the Mexican army. With Davy Crockett, Jim Bowie, and Sam Houston, among others, Emily became the subject of myth, legend, and elaborated fact.

But what really happened? Did Emily West Morgan seduce Santa Anna, so the Texans could encircle the camp? Was the Yellow Rose a woman of easy virtue? Did she save Texas?

We know that Emily West was in her thirties, a freeborn mulatto from Connecticut who made her living as a housekeeper. We also know that, in her day, a person of mixed ancestry or a lightly skinned black was called a *high yellow*—and if the person was a beautiful woman, she might be referred to as a *yellow rose*. What's more, she could read and write and do

A white man could visit a black brothel, but a black man could expect to be severely beaten, tarred and feathered, or hung if he tried to do business with a white woman. This establishment was run by Madam Sperber. COURTESY KENNETH SPENCER RESEARCH LIBRARY, UNIVERSITY OF KANSAS LIBRARIES, JOSEPH J. PENNELL COLLECTION.

some math. Her education was highly unusual for the time. That she was a beautiful woman, everyone seemed to agree. She may have wanted to broaden her horizons. Perhaps she had a desperate need for money. For whatever reason, Emily indentured herself to James Morgan. He was an entrepreneur with business dealings in the colony of Texas. Emily agreed to work as a housekeeper for one year for $100. Morgan would pay her passage to and from Texas. Because Emily was considered black, there could be complications. She took Morgan's last name as a matter of course and for her protection. This was a common practice, not only for slaves but also for bond servants during their indenture. Thus in Texas she would be known as Emily Morgan. Many thought of her as one of Morgan's slaves, not knowing she had freeborn papers and a contract.

The question that many ask is, was the title of "housekeeper" a

Emily West's freeborn papers included this "passport" acknowledging her status as a "free woman," having emigrated to Texas from New York.

COURTESY TEXAS STATE LIBRARY AND ARCHIVES COMMISSION.

euphemism for prostitute? Was she Morgan's mistress? Did she go to Texas to be a prostitute as implied in folklore? All good questions. In some Texas settlements, there were many men and few women, so female companionship was at a premium. Prostitution would have been a lucrative business move for her (and for Morgan if he was sharing in the profits). And it would have worked handily into the legend. Bawdy girls were in demand, but so were women who could cook, clean house, and perform household duties for work-worn men and women. James Morgan was a wheeler-dealer with his fingers in a number of financial pies. He was developing his own plantation, selling real estate, and growing businesses. He was also an enthusiastic supporter of the new republic. He led an army and was made a general. He owned more than thirty slaves on his plantation, but he seems to have treated Emily fairly. She might have been a prostitute, but there isn't enough evidence to prove it.

Emily's first job was at a hotel, a likely place for a housekeeper or a prostitute. Being both literate and knowing basic math probably made her a business asset for Morgan at the hotel. As the war grew closer to New Washington, the hotel was full every night. Literally thousands of Texans were fleeing from the Mexican forces creeping nearer. The news had not been good from the Alamo and Goliad. Prices for goods and services skyrocketed. A drink of whiskey was a quarter. A bed for the night was a dollar. Emily was busy, and Morgan reaped a windfall.

For some reason, Emily did not flee with the others when Santa Anna's forces approached. She stayed in New Washington until it was too late. Perhaps she didn't understand the gravity of the times. It was bad luck, but she was captured by the Mexican army. Santa Anna was a notorious womanizer and was known for raping captured women. She was pretty and was put in his bawdy "holding pen." Because he had other women in his lineup and a battle to fight, he apparently had not gotten around to looking at the current bevy of captured females from the local countryside or New Washington. With the other captured women, Emily was put in the custody of the army's laundry ladies, so the president could look them over later. On the outskirts of New Washington, Santa Anna pitched camp almost on top of the Texans, where the battle would soon be fought. Both he and his army were tired from the long march, and he decided they needed a siesta. A bad choice. After the battles he'd won against the rebels, he felt this confrontation would be another victory against some backwoods hicks. Also, his arrogant boldness in making camp so close to the enemy would, he felt, give him a psychological advantage. Who were these Texans anyway? He called for the mixed-blood woman previously scheduled to entertain him during his afternoon rest period. Because Emily was of mixed blood, too, she was grabbed by mistake, and the legend was born. Savoring his past victories, wine, and opium, Santa Anna wasn't thinking clearly. As we know, he grossly underestimated the rebels.

Had the Mexican army defeated the Texans, Emily might, at some point, have become a victim of Santa Anna's bedroom lust. Instead, the battle was over almost before it started. When the shooting started, Emily, along with the other laundry ladies, took cover so a stray bullet wouldn't catch them. Likely she heard more of the battle than she saw. There's a good chance that she never even saw the supreme leader, unless he galloped past her in his silken undies, trying to effect an ignoble escape while his men surrendered. Emily was near the battlefront but not with the general. After the Texans' victory, she surely took a deep breath and headed back to the hotel, so she could catch up on the work she had missed during her incarceration.

So how did Emily West Morgan, housekeeper or prostitute, become Texas' most famous siren, the Yellow Rose? When she had completed her year as a bond servant, she left Texas and sailed back to New England. By 1840 there is no census record of her in Connecticut. Emily West simply drops out of history. However, her reputation in the republic grew exponentially. Because she was at or near the right place at the right time, it appears that people simply assumed that she was the woman with Santa Anna. She was a woman they could put a name to. She was captured by the Mexicans, after all, and she was pretty, and Santa Anna had been with a mulatto. Therefore, it must have been Emily. James Morgan had been a patriot in the battle, and Emily was his servant; therefore, again, she must have been a patriot, too. True, she was no longer in Texas to verify the facts; thus, Texas logic concludes, she must have been with Santa Anna, and she was the Yellow Rose. By association, the assumptions grew, and Emily wasn't there to contradict the story.

Yellow Rose of Texas: The Song

From the University of Texas archives, this early version (perhaps the original version) of *The Yellow Rose of Texas* is sung from the point of view of an African American and makes no mention of the republic's fight for independence. The spelling is rustic and the word choices chafe at modern ears, but the song remains plaintive.

The Yellow Rose of Texas

There's a yellow rose in Texas,
that I am going to see,
No other darky knows her,
no darky only me
She cryed so when I left her
it like to broke my heart,
And if I ever find her,
we nevermore will part.

Chorus:
She's the sweetest rose of color
this darky ever knew,
Her eyes are bright as diamonds,
they sparkle like the dew;
You may talk about your Dearest May,
and sing of Rosa Lee,
But the Yellow Rose of Texas
is the only girl for me.

When the Rio Grande is flowing,
the starry skies are bright,
She walks along the river
in the quite summer night:
She thinks if I remember,
when we parted long ago,
I promised to come back again,
and not to leave her so.
[Chorus]

Oh now I'm going to find her,
for my heart is full of woe,
And we'll sing the songs togeather,
that we sung so long ago
We'll play the bango gaily,
and we'll sing the songs of yore,
And the Yellow Rose of Texas
shall be mine forevermore.
[Chorus]

Then the local slaves started singing a song about a mulatto slave girl who turned the tides of war for the Texans. It had a rather tight set of lyrics that was catchy and easy to learn. It became a favorite among the workers. She was, they believed, a slave who had done great things, and they could relate to her. The song soon gained in popularity and became a favorite in taverns and bars on the South Texas coast. The song was called *The Yellow Rose of Texas* or *Emily, the Maid of Morgan's Point* (named after James Morgan). Before long, the title *The Yellow Rose of Texas* seemed to edge out *Emily, the Maid of Morgan's Point* because the latter didn't have the word Texas in it. Texans celebrated the song about the girl who seduced Santa Anna for Texas. The song was presented to Sam Houston, who loved it because it glorified the revolution. Sam Houston had a mythic feeling for Texas and supported anything, tall tales or the truth, as long as it promoted the Texas war for independence.

Some scholars think that James Morgan might have given the song to Houston. Morgan was directly connected with Emily, and that association, true or not, was good for his business. He was a shameless promoter of his projects, and Emily had played a part in that. The British writer William Bollaert visited Texas and became good friends with James Morgan. Morgan gave Bollaert his "unique" slant on the battle. His account wasn't factual, but Morgan and the Texans looked very good. It was an interesting piece of revisionist history. In *William Bollaert's Texas*, Bollaert didn't bother to check the facts and instead merely took Morgan's word. He wrote about the battle of San Jacinto, Morgan-style. Bollaert boldly proclaims that the battle "Was probably lost to the Mexicans . . . [except for] the influence of a Mullatta girl belonging to Col. Morgan who was closeted in the tent with General Santana at the time the [battle] cry was made."

The popularity of the song spread across Texas and into other states. It remains a favorite even today, although some of the words have been changed. Emily probably never knew a song had been written about her or that the state of Texas considered her a hero. ⇥

CHAPTER NINE

DORA B. TOPHAM

Madam Belle London

In December 1908, Salt Lake City law enforcement gave notice: All bawdy girls, prostitutes, and madams have until 4:00 a.m. to turn off their red lights, or else! Purveyors of flesh, you have three options: Leave town, go to jail, or relocate to the new "Stockade."

The Stockade was a city-sanctioned whore-block in downtown Salt Lake City, Block 64 to be precise. It was located at 1st and 2nd South and 5th and 6th West Streets. All prostitution would be confined to this singular location. This block of sin, as it was sometimes called, would be run by none other than the infamous madam and businesswoman from Ogden, Utah, Mrs. Dora B. Topham, aka Madam Belle London. Dora Topham was a successful madam, rich in her own right, who controlled Electric Alley and Two-bit Street and a dozen other businesses and whorehouses in Ogden, north of Salt Lake City. To manage their radical experiment, the conservative Mormon town fathers wanted someone with experience, both literally and figuratively.

In order to clean up their fair city, Mayor Bransford and the Salt Lake City Council decided it would be wise to put all their rotten bawdy eggs

Madam Dora Topham looked like a strict schoolteacher, but she was one of the richest, most successful madams in the West. She considered herself a reformer of the profession.

in one basket. Get rid of all the pockets of prostitution, the brothels, the streetwalkers, the lewd antics, and the door-step exhibitionists in one fell swoop. Mayor Bransford said, "I propose to take these women from the business section of the city and put them in a district which will be one of the best, if not the very best, regulated districts in the country." In other words, isolate prostitution in one location, control it, tax it, and contain it. The out-of-sight out-of-mind philosophy . . . but don't forget to pay your fees to city hall. This wasn't the first time Salt Lake City had tried to sweep the flesh trade from the so-called City of the Saints. No previous attempts had been successful. But many agreed that confining prostitution in a stockade might work. Lewd girls would be able to go off-site and live if they wanted to, but they could only do business within the compound. And who was best qualified to run a morally corrupt business? An honest man, certainly not! It could only be managed by a fallen, morally corrupt woman . . . yet someone they could trust. This woman would have to have good business sense, a proven track record, a disregard for decent morality, and a willingness to answer to the mayor and city council. After examining her unwritten curriculum vitae, Dora Topham was the mayor's woman . . . or madam as the case might be. It didn't hurt her portfolio, either, that she was wealthy enough not to need the job and could buy or sell nearly any one of the town council. This particular woman, Madam Dora, happened to be worth more than half a million dollars, a very hefty sum in her day. More important to Dora, she figured this gig could make her a lot more money. It was like a legal monopoly, so she dealt herself in.

Before the Stockade proposal, city fathers and businessmen noticed that property values near the red light district were deteriorating. Furthermore, it was embarrassing that a predominantly Mormon community should have prostitution so boldly displayed near the downtown area. Some streetwalkers were too bold. They solicited honest men who were walking with their families. Such immoral behavior could not be tolerated. It was a violation of moral decency. To fight the problem, raids and arrests were made. Even a "prostitution record" was instituted, a plan endorsed by both law enforcement and the Salt Lake City Council. Those charged with soliciting or caught during a raid could be traced, then jailed, heavily fined, or sent out of town. Madams of brothels were also required to keep the names and the records of their inmates. A fine of $10 a month was also levied on each working girl. Such actions made a dent in the bawdy trade but did not extinguish it.

In spite of the conservative Latter-day Saint influence, Salt Lake City had had a long battle with prostitution. The Mormon influence was strongly felt, but that alone wasn't enough to keep the city pure. Prostitution first came to prominence in 1858 during the Utah War when the U.S. Army established Camp Floyd southeast of the city. Brothels sprang up, and prostitutes quickly flocked near the camp to prey on the soldiers who were far from home and lonely. After the soldiers left, many of the women thought that the mountain air was healthy, so they gravitated toward the cities, some established by the Mormons and others by the "Gentiles." Ogden was a Gentile city, and there were a number of working girls plying their trade there, including Belle London. Salt Lake had a number of bold and colorful madams who drew a fair patronage, especially from the large number of non-Mormons in the valley. Kate Flint, Lou Wallace, and Miss Helen Blazes were a few who were in and out of court and had police records. There are historical accounts of police raids and legal proceedings—and embarrassing situations when prominent people were caught with their pants down.

Nevertheless, in communities with a high population of Mormons, prostitution numbers were lower per capita. But any was too many for proper sensibilities. Because the business was so frowned upon, the agreement between a conservative Mormon mayor and whoremonger Madam Dora B. Topham remains as one of the strangest business deals in Great Basin history. It must have seemed a bit odd to the casual observer that the mayor would recruit such management talent. But Dora had never rocked the political machine or made a public scene like local Salt Lake madams had. Dora had a thriving business in Ogden with a highly successful brothel, but she didn't make waves. Her business expanded from a single brothel to Electric Alley, another brothel in Ogden that was near an ice cream parlor. She bought and expanded the Livingston Confectionery two years later. She also purchased the Palace Ballard Hall, the Gasberg Building, and another place on 25th Street. Each was managed carefully and turned a tidy profit. Her business expansion strategies were astute.

Salt Lake City Councilman L. D. Martin was one who supported the Stockade proposal.

She had proved to be one of the most skilled businesswomen in the latter part of the nineteenth century, and would likely be running a Fortune 500 company today. She was known to be strict, but honest. It's obvious that she was a thorough money manager. She had a good eye for opportunity and knew good investments when she saw them.

With the support of the city council and fifty successful businessmen, the mayor brought Dora to Salt Lake. Businessmen were relieved to learn that Dora thought the campaign strategy of isolating prostitution could be successful. She also argued that this move would keep prostitution from spreading, which is what the community leaders wanted to hear. Because there had been so much bickering among the local prostitutes and madams in Salt Lake, Bransford felt that the Stockade concept would work better if a complete outsider ran it. Thus the two were strange bedfellows: the conservative mayor who hated prostitution and the soiled dove who was a stone-cold businesswoman. To avoid as much official involvement as he could, the mayor had Dora do most of the groundwork for the project. She formed a corporation called the Citizens Investment Company and raised several hundred thousand dollars. Under Dora's organization, the company issued 2,500 shares of stock at $100 a share and gave the Salt Lake Security and Trust Company a trust deed to insure the bonds. Dora owned 1,260 shares and controlled another 1,200 as trustee. It was rumored that she said, "I risk my money; the mayor risks re-election."

Dora purchased the land, noting that it was near three railroads and away from schools. There would be only three outside entries and no windows facing the street. There would be 100 brick cribs that would each be ten feet square. Inside each crib would be a window and a door, an enamel bed, a nightstand with a washbasin, and a chair. A working girl would furnish her own linen and pay $1 to $4 a day for rent. There were parlor houses in the Stockade, too. Parlor house rent started at $175 a month. Drinking establishments were another important revenue stream. In addition to the main doors, there were secret doors for important people who wanted to visit anonymously.

Thanks to Dora Topham's management, the plans were finalized, and the building was constructed in months. Ground was broken in the summer of 1908, and the building was completed by the following winter. It may

Venereal Disease through the Ages

Today we know there are at least twenty different types of venereal disease. While ancient cultures tended to look at venereal affliction as one malady, they were aware that there was a direct connection between the sex act and an awful disease. The ancient Egyptians treated this infection with garlic, ground cow horn, and scents. There is also evidence they invented the condom for the express purpose of preventing the transfer of disease. Ancient Babylon thought that extensive washing would prevent and cure the disease. Ancient Greek writers were aware that sexual intimacy transmitted disease; treatment and prevention in such a sexually active culture was a concern. Baths and oils were used. Pliny also mentions using condoms.

The Indian *Sushruta Samhita*, a Sanskrit text about surgery written between 300 and 400 B.C., describes venereal disease. It also suggests traditional medicines, including a mercury salve (which was one of the few semi-effective treatments). Similar observations were made in the *Huang-Ti Nei-Ching (The Yellow Emperor's Classic on Internal Medicine)*. Chinese physicians believed the illness shifted a victim's body out of balance, and they treated the patient with herbs and acupuncture.

In Europe during the Middle Ages, virulent strains of syphilis broke out. The victims would develop pustules covering their bodies. The person would ache and hurt, while inside the disease was attacking the nervous system and organs. Death often occurred in a few months. These horrible epidemics

have been the only time the city government of Salt Lake knowingly employed a madam to work for the municipality. In the photos we have of Dora, she looks studious and businesslike, more like a schoolmarm than a madam. For Dora, prostitution was a business, and she ran it that way.

She considered herself a prostitution reformer, making it better for all concerned. It was a high turnover business. In an interview with a reporter for the *Herald-Republican* (July 1, 1909), Dora B. Topham said:

I'm a business woman; I'm a good manager . . . . I don't like [prostitution] I abhor it. My conscience—yes, I have a conscience—has troubled me about it a good many times. I can do this much: I can make this business as clean as it is possible for such a business as this killed like the plague; Holy Roman emperors, popes, cardinals, royalty, and kings fell victim along with the common folk. Venereal diseases were sometimes confused with leprosy, and the infected were rounded up and put in leper-like V.D. colonies. Removing the problem seemed the best way to cure the disease. For example, in 1498, the French king ordered those with venereal disease to leave Paris within one day, or they would be executed. In some areas, prostitutes would be inspected and sent away if they appeared infected. This task was sometimes performed by midwives.

By the ninetheenth century, little had changed. Condoms were known to fight disease, but it wasn't until the latter part of the 1800s that condoms were readily available, though still not widely used. There was a cottage industry in home remedies. Plant poultices were used: sassafras, guaiac tree, sarsaparilla. Mercury was common, too. Then in 1928, Scottish scientist Alexander Fleming noticed that penicillium mold had killed bacteria in a petri dish in his lab. He published a report in the *British Journal of Experimental Pathology,* but it garnered little attention. So the discovery languished until 1938 when biochemist Ernst Chain stumbled on Fleming's paper. Finding the most effective strain of the mold and reproducing it in usable quantities proved difficult. Soon, however, World War II provided the push (and funding) to find a cure for wound infections, and researchers figured out how to mass produce penicillin. By the end of the war, U.S. pharmaceuticals were producing over 600 billion doses of penicillin each month. Venereal disease had met its match.

to be, and I can persuade a great many girls who are just starting to lead a life of shame to travel other paths.

To minimize this problem, she hired only women who wanted to be in the profession, not young teens. She had a reputation for sending girls away, back to their parents or husbands, if she felt they were not suited for the bawdy life. Careful hiring meant less turnover, and that was good for business. Before she hired a girl, she was given a medical check to make sure she was free of disease and healthy. Dora also ran a small hospital and gave her employees medical care—this included treatment (as archaic as it was then) for venereal disease.

Before the building was complete, Dora personally visited every brothel and prostitute she could find in the city and invited them to come to the Stockade. She argued the advantages: reasonable rent, and they could, for the most part, avoid the hassle of busts and raids. (This didn't work quite as well as planned, but by nineteenth-century prostitute standards, the Stockade was mostly hassle free if you were a working girl.) Dora was able to talk some of the girls into coming to her establishment, but not as many as she hoped. A lot of independent women and madams would have nothing to do with her—something she had not planned for. Neither she nor the city council anticipated the resistance they faced. Even with threats and strong-arm tactics by law enforcement, recruits were hard won. Understandably, successful businesses, especially if they owned their own properties or liked their locations, were reluctant to move. Some women did not like the idea of being lumped together in one large conglomerate. Untrusting by nature, they felt the plan might not work. The added threat of raids from the police didn't seem to be as troubling as Dora had originally thought. Besides, some of the smaller operations had so far escaped notice by the police, and they felt secure. They saw no reason to move. Dora had a good reputation among her peers, so few doubted her sincerity, but it was not an easy sell. Dora Topham's famous statement to the women she encountered was, "I will protect you with my life, if need be. I know what I am talking about. This place will not be molested."

She even offered free rent for a short time to everyone who came over, but there were still vacancies after the proverbial ribbon was cut. To ensure profits and financial solvency, Dora took matters into her own hands. She had a healthy portion of her own money in the venture and wasn't about to let it flounder. Because she could not fill the Stockade with local women, she recruited. The Stockade was supposed to cut down on prostitution by isolating it into one block. But as Dora discovered, she could not force independent working women to come into the Stockade. Instead, she advertised nationally, calling for prostitutes to come to Salt Lake and work at a fancy new whorehouse, a concept called the Stockade. Before long, perhaps half of her employees were from out of town. Yes, prostitution was heavily isolated on Block 64, but freelancers were still working around the city. Shortly, the number of prostitutes in Salt Lake City had dramatically increased. This was not part of the mayor's plan.

From 1908 to 1911, the Stockade was busy. Dora's office was located off the north entrance. The inmates of the Stockade were a mixed racial group. Most of the parlor houses were for higher-class white women, although there was one lower-end black parlor house. According to an article in the September 4, 1910, *Herald Republican,* one place had several Japanese girls. There were also several Latino prostitutes. Most of the Stockade security force were off-duty Salt Lake City policemen. There was even a cell in case a patron got sloppy drunk or out of control and needed to sleep it off. In addition, a handy Chinese opium vendor sold pipe dreams. There were eating places, tobacco stores, saloons, and a dance floor. Each girl was charged rent by the day, and beer was $1 a bottle. In theory, each girl had to be examined by a doctor every ten days. In the early stages of Dora's planning, medical exams and care were to be free. As it turned out, most women got charged a dollar a visit, including regular, mandatory venereal examinations. Many girls did not want to sleep in their cribs, so they rented a room for $4 or $5 a week somewhere nearby. Each girl also paid a "fine" for the police. Some of these fine-print details were not discussed when a woman moved into the Stockade, and they became a source of friction. Nevertheless, the police fine must have worked. According to *Annual Reports of Officers of Salt Lake City,* prostitution arrests dropped from a little over 1,000 a year to only a handful.

The police did raid from time to time to keep the public happy or to investigate complaints, but their efforts were perfunctory. Unless a crime was committed, the law enforcement machine of Salt Lake City mostly ignored the giant, brick bordello.

Inside the Stockade, life was decidedly risqué. A girl who was not otherwise occupied with a client might sit in her window, or on her doorstep, to tempt a prospective John for a date. Bouncers at each door kept out decent women and the underaged or the uncontrolled drunks. There was also an alarm so that in the event of a raid everyone was warned and the power would go out.

In 1909, a particular incident spelled the beginning of the end for this "social" experiment in Mormon Territory. In spite of management's best efforts to keep out the underaged, a boy by the name of Dogney Gray managed to get past the guard at the door and was corrupted by one of the working girls. Opposition had already grown against the great experiment, but this was a deal breaker. It was obvious the Stockade hadn't worked. There were more working girls than ever. State lawmakers began challenging the Stockade by firming up laws against any landowner who allowed prostitution. A group called the Civic Betterment League filed papers against Dora and her working girls. Public sympathy was quickly eroding. One member of the league, Lorenzo Haddock, said, "It is a simple case of whether Salt Lake shall be known as the most depraved city in the country with regard to its fostering and protecting the social evil or whether we shall have a city that is known as moral and decent and law abiding." As the manager and primary stockholder, Dora Topham naturally drew the first and most direct salvos. The citizens demanded closure. While the Salt Lake police did not respond to public demand, the Salt Lake county sheriff did. The sheriff's office openly crusaded against her. These were some rocky legal times, but Dora managed to keep the thriving brick brothel open.

More public outcry was heard. The public and legal pressure culminated in charges against Dora B. Topham for soliciting and corrupting young Dogney's morals. Because she was the one in charge, she was the one wearing the moral-indecency target on her back. She had an expensive defense, but it was not enough. Not surprisingly, Dora was found guilty and sentenced to eighteen years in prison. Later, the Utah Supreme Court reversed the decision of the lower court. She was free, but the incident had soured her on the Stockade, Salt Lake City, and its municipal government. She also argued that some of the evidence used against her was manufactured by the police department.

Washing her hands of the experiment, she proclaimed that on September 28, 1911, the Stockade would be closed. She returned to Ogden. The people of Salt Lake had won. Not long after she closed the brick house down, the city destroyed the building. It was as if razing the block would show the world it had never been there.

We know about Dora's public life in Salt Lake and Ogden because she was involved in public matters. However, we know very little about her personal and private affairs. She kept her personal life private. She was very enigmatic about her history. What we've gleaned are only fragments

Radical Temperance campaigner Carrie Nation, who used a hatchet to damage property in taverns, moved society toward Prohibition and other "moral reforms." Tolerance for prostitution gradually waned. COURTESY SOUTH DAKOTA STATE HISTORICAL SOCIETY.

here and there. She was born in either Illinois or Kentucky around 1865. Her name might have been Adora Long. In the late 1870s, she probably worked as a bawd in Colorado. In the early 1890s, she moved to thriving Ogden, Utah, where she wed Thomas Topham. She had a child in 1896 in Nebraska. Her marriage to Thomas likely soured around 1899; the census then indicates that she lived alone. (That same year, Thomas was accused of murdering a man named Charles Wessler, tried, and acquitted.) In 1902, they divorced and she received alimony. After her legal problems in Salt Lake, she wanted to focus on raising her daughter (she might have had another daughter by now) and to tend to her other business interests. Soured on Utah, she liquidated her businesses and moved to California. She continued raising her family and setting up other businesses. In 1925, she was helping one of her employees tow a stalled car with her own vehicle. An accident occurred, and she was crushed between the two vehicles. Dora B. Topham, Madame Belle London, died five days later. ⇥

CHAPTER TEN

MOLLY B'DAM

Maggie Hall Was
a Good Catholic Girl

E ven though she was a whore, Molly B'Dam was a good lady, if
there's a hint of truth in the legends and stories that surround her.
Most mythologies about whores' "hearts of gold" are just stories.
Some of Molly's acts of kindness, however, are verifiable—it seems
she was a kind, giving woman. But, like so many western characters,
occasionally the legend overshadows the real person, and fact and fiction
get twisted. Molly was well liked by the community, even by some of the
housewives. Kind, yes, but Molly was also a shrewd businesswoman who
knew how to hang on to her money. She was also a clever marketer, as
Molly and her infamous bathtub adventures prove.

A miner in the 1880s observed that Molly had "an uncommonly
ravishing personality. Her face gave no evidence of her disposition, her
clothes no hint of her profession . . . [Molly] had an atmosphere of re-
finement and culture." She was not one of the rougher women of the
settlements, but rather possessed some lady-like traits.

Maggie Hall was born to a Protestant father and a Roman Catholic mother on December 26, 1853, in Dublin, Ireland. Maggie grew into a beautiful young girl, and her parents doted on her. She was well educated and familiar with the classics. She could quote Shakespeare, Dante, and Milton verbatim, among other poets. She also knew her Bible. She was a popular girl who made friends easily and liked to laugh. She had thick blonde hair and deep blue eyes. As she matured, Maggie was nearly five feet, six inches tall with a gorgeous figure. She attracted many of the local boys, some with marriage proposals. Maggie, however, had a wanderlust, and she felt confined in Ireland. Like the wild geese, she longed for new places, and Ireland could not hold her. She wanted to go to the United States where she felt she would have greater opportunities.

When she was twenty years old, she boarded a ship alone for New York City to seek her fortune. It was a tearful parting. Her parents begged her not to leave, but Maggie was anything if not strong willed. It would be the last time the Halls would see their daughter. Maggie was amazed at how large New York was. She had enough money put away so she could live for a while, but she found little opportunity in the big city—especially if one was Irish. When her money ran out, she took a job in a drinking establishment as a barmaid. She quickly found it necessary to educate her customers—all she was selling was drinks. Her cheerful manner and her happy personality made Molly a hit with the customers as well as with management. She was a devout Catholic who went to mass and confession frequently. She worked as a barmaid for more than a year, but one cold winter afternoon, her life would change, and there would be no coming back.

The Irish lass, who had taken so many men's hearts, fell in love at first sight. She could have almost any man, but she chose this one. He was well dressed, good looking, and had charming manners. His name was Burdan (we don't know his first name), and he was the son of a wealthy family. After their third meeting, he proposed marriage. Maggie insisted that they be married in the Catholic Church, but he insisted that they get married right away. Disappointed but so in love, she conceded. Burdan woke up a city official he knew who promptly married the couple. He took Maggie back to his luxurious apartment for their honeymoon. Maggie had never seen such opulence.

Working Girls on Army Posts

As a rule, working girls were not officially allowed on U.S. Army bases; however, such regulations did not stop the flow of trade. Company commanders frequently sidestepped or blinked at official mandates. Regulations allowed a post to hire laundresses to wash the men's clothes. While there were certainly honest women in the laundry trade (often enlisted men's wives), a good number did a thriving business after hours. Perhaps it was more than coincidental that laundress quarters were often near the enlisted men's barracks. On the frontier, a laundress was a euphemism for an army whore.

Like the laundry women, the army also hired "nurses," who did a thriving business in the venal arts, too. According to the *Military Laws and Rules and Regulations for the Army of the United States*, the qualifications

69. FORT LARAMIE.

were few. "These women [could not be] infected by the venereal disease" or they were dismissed.

A post also needed a general store, but the army wasn't interested in daily mercantile management. Thus the army contracted a store, called the sutler's store, to a private concern. While the store was subject to military regulations, it wasn't uncommon for the proprietor to take liberties if the post commander was lax or disinterested. In addition to selling pocket watches, tobacco, pocket knives, and shaving gear, many store managers branched out into more lucrative ventures. Sometimes women under the watchful eye of sutler store management would set up shop on the premises. At other times, the store would regulate the extracurricular services of the laundry women. As long as the activities were low profile and didn't draw attention, some officers felt this was the best of several evils because the men were less inclined to stray from the fort.

While there was a pretense to follow regulations, West Point etiquette was quickly replaced by frontier pragmatism. As a case in point, Captain John G. Bourke was traveling through dangerous country with a group of soldiers. Bourke recorded in his diary that his sense of military propriety was offended because a chief clerk was traveling with Mollie Shepherd, a well-known prostitute. He felt this was stepping over the line. This job proved a bad choice for Mollie. The small band was attacked by Indians, and Mollie was killed. Bourke mentions her in his journal, but because Mollie was a working girl, she was hardly mentioned in the official report.

Army forts were a natural market for working girls on the frontier. The amenities at Fort Laramie, Wyoming, shown here in 1870, included a nearby hog ranch.
COURTESY OF U.S. GEOLOGICAL SURVEY, PHOTOGRAPH BY W. H. JACKSON.

It did surprise her, though, when her new husband told her that she would need to change her name. Maggie was all too common, and Irish, and would not do for his wife. Instead, he told her that the name he had chosen for her was Molly. He also told his new bride that they would need to keep their marriage a secret. His parents were very proper and would never allow their son to marry an Irish woman, let alone a barmaid. Burdan explained that he received a generous allowance from his family, but he would risk losing their financial support if they discovered he'd married beneath himself.

For several months they lived in luxury, but Burdan's parents eventually found out, and he was cut off financially. The young couple moved from place to place, never paying their bills. Finally, one day with his head on Molly's lap, he confessed that he was deeply in debt and was in danger of being beaten, maybe killed. Not only did he owe a number of apartment houses for past rent and was spending money he did not have, he was also a gambler, a poor one, who owed great sums to friends and associates. He feared for his well-being if he didn't pay his gambling debts soon. He could see no way out . . . except one.

He told Molly that she was a beautiful and a desirable woman and that he loved her. His friends and associates, he commented, had all noticed her—how could they not. He blatantly suggested that if she would sleep with one of his friends, it would relieve a very pressing debt. Molly had a temper and was understandably insulted by such an indecent proposal. Burdan persisted and begged, and finally Molly reluctantly consented to sleeping with her husband's friends. She felt cheap and tawdry, but she did it because she loved him. Molly was a moral woman, a practicing Catholic, and she was certain she'd committed a serious sin . . . in love or not.

However, it didn't stop.

Burdan's debts were great, and over time he brought a string of men to sleep with his wife. Molly was incensed and felt used. With a haunting conscience, she crept to confession and told the priest about what she had done. The priest told her that she must stop her immoral behavior immediately or her soul would be in grave peril. That night, she explained this to her husband, but he seemed indifferent to her pleas. He continued to prostitute his lovely bride to his associates to pay his debts. Later, burdened with guilt, she returned to the confessional. To her horror, the priest excommunicated her from the Catholic Church. For a deeply religious girl, this was the cruelest blow of all. She felt she'd been betrayed by the two things she loved most. Certain that she was damned forever and would be sent to hell, Molly felt she had nothing to lose. She continued her sordid life, but she noticed that her love for her husband was fading, and she grew to despise him. He used her in a malicious way. She decided to leave him and seek her fortune in the West. Molly saved money until she had a bankroll, and then she left. She was twenty-four years old, and for the first time in her life, she would work for herself. She visited or worked in several large cities, Chicago and San Francisco among them, and wandered over a good part of the West. She liked to travel. Her main interest and specialty, though, was boomtowns, because a lot of money could be made there. She was good at her job, and she charged outrageous prices for her services.

When she was nearly thirty years old and well seasoned in her trade, she heard of a huge strike in northern Idaho near Coeur d'Alene. Molly decided to travel to a town called Murray and set up business. The Molly B'Dam legend has both Calamity Jane and Molly leaving for Deadwood at the same time, both bound for Murray and the gold fields. When Calamity saw Molly, as the story goes, she got off at the next station and headed back to Dakota Territory. Molly was so beautiful, Calamity claimed, she herself would get very little business in Idaho.

But the legend of her travels into the gold fields doesn't stop here. While her exploits seem nonpareil, there is a core of truth in the next Molly story—it's the frills we question. In 1884, she rode the train from Deadwood into Montana Territory. The rest of the journey had to be taken either on foot or horseback. Molly, according to folklore, bought a handsome black stallion and a pack animal to carry her wardrobe. She joined a train of eager gold hunters and headed west toward Coeur d'Alene, specifically Murray, Idaho. Gold fever had struck the region, and thousands had dreams of wealth. Those with enough money bought a horse. Others walked, carrying or pulling their gear. It was a difficult trek, especially for those without a mount. Since winter was threatening in the high country, there was a sense of urgency to pick up the pace. As they went up Thompson Pass (which is nearly 7,000 feet above sea level),

Murray, Idaho, was a boomtown when Molly hung up her shingle. It was the place she called home.

a severe blizzard hit as they were crossing the summit. In spite of the blinding weather and night coming on, most of the train decided to make a mad rush to safety down the west side of the pass. Murray was only seven miles away. But Molly noticed that a mother with a small child had fallen behind in the snow. She noted earlier that neither one was dressed for the cold weather. Rather than seek her own safety, Molly went back and found the pair and led them to a crude shelter she had seen earlier. Dressing the freezing mother and child in her elegant furs, Molly managed to get a fire started, warming the hut against the night. She wanted to make a dash for Murray, but she didn't think the two were ready to travel. She told some of the stragglers in the train that she was going to spend the night on the mountain with her new friends. She'd be in Murray in the morning.

The townspeople were understandably worried about the woman on the black horse and the mother and her child. Speculation was they'd not survive the night. The blizzard was too strong and visibility poor, so no search party was attempted. The next morning, while some of the men were organizing a trip back up Thompson's Pass, a tall woman holding a child rode into town with another woman clinging to her on back of the saddle. She dropped the mother and child, oddly dressed in her expensive furs, at a cabin so they could get warm and be fed, insisting they send the bill to her. One legend has the entire town rushing out to meet and congratulate Molly. An Irishman who would become one of her best friends apparently helped her off her horse. He identified himself as Phil O'Rourke. She introduced herself as Molly Burdan. Because of her brogue he thought she said her name was "Molly B'Dam!" He laughed, and the name stuck. From that time forth, she was Molly B'Dam to one and all. She laughed about it and liked her new name, or so the legend goes.

Some of the men tried to take her luggage to a cabin. However, she insisted that she be taken to Cabin Number One. This was a euphemism. It meant she was a prostitute, and she'd stay where prostitutes stayed—not where decent women had lodging. Molly liked this town (which at statehood was bigger than Boise), and she wanted to stay. Did she rescue the two from a bad situation? Very likely. Was it cold and snowing? Probably. Was the horse black, was there a packhorse, did the mother and child wear her furs to stay warm, did she stay all night on the mountain, did she ask for a prostitute's cabin? Those answers are up for grabs. How much is real and how much has been spun after her death is difficult to say.

She got along with the residents, though, including "honest" women. And she was well liked. When she fell ill, decent women of the town were said to have sat by her bed. This may have happened, but it's hard to know to what extent. A lot of mythology has been woven in with the truth, making her a folk hero. Nevertheless, this kind treatment for a whore didn't happen very often. If she really rescued a mother and child, it might have wiped away some of her professional taint. She dressed well in expensive clothes; she didn't dress like a whore. This would have helped, too. The men liked her, and she was fair and honest. It was said that Molly would stand a hungry man or a family to a meal and had grubstaked more than a handful of men. She was also known for clothing the women and children of struggling miners. Molly attended a Protestant church since the Catholic Church had excommunicated her.

She was kind, but she wasn't cheap. The old stories claim that she charged a large price for her favors. Indeed, she was a very expensive evening and always had been. Some miners worked, according to lore, for half a year to be able to spend a night with her. Eventually, she added girls to her establishment and became a successful madam. Unlike many madams, however, people claimed that Molly was fair and would not tolerate her girls stealing money from a client, no matter how drunk he was. When one of her girls stole the poke of a miner named Lightning, she found the thief and made sure the John got his money back. When Lightning fell ill, reportedly Molly took food and supplies up to his shack. Molly's specialty, however, was her erotic bathing. She called them "cleanup baths," and clean up she did.

When word got around that Molly was going to do one of her baths, excitement flared throughout the town. Miners counted their nuggets and gold dust to see if they had enough. This was not something a crusty miner wanted to miss if he could help it—or afford it. The rules of the game went something like this. Each man had to put so much gold dust in the tub, until the bottom was completely covered. If a man didn't put enough dust in the tub, or his pouch ran dry, he'd have to leave. The rest stood around and watched. When Molly figured the bottom of the tub was sufficiently covered, she'd come out, her hair tucked up, disrobe, and climb into the expensive tub. If a man got really generous and dumped in some more dust, he got to scrub her back. If he got *really* generous, she'd let him climb into the tub and scrub her back. Over the years there were variations on the bathtub scenario, but it always included a disrobed Molly and a lot of gold dust. In good weather, this lusty event took place in Paradise Alley, alfresco. When she was in the tub, Molly would sing and tell jokes and stories.

Molly's business thrived, and she remained good friends with Phil O'Rourke. She donated to civic causes and was respected by those on both sides of the track. In 1886, a tragedy struck Murray. A man rode into town, drank some whiskey, and tumbled over dead. He was quickly diagnosed with smallpox. The town was facing an epidemic. Before long, there were several dozen fatalities from this dreaded disease. Fearing they might be next, the townspeople retreated to their homes to ride out the epidemic. Supposedly, there was a doctor in town, but he wasn't much use. No one

Molly was laid to rest in Murray, Idaho. This wooden grave marker was later replaced by a headstone.

knew how to fight the infection. According to legend, Molly rallied the town, which had not been proactive in helping the sick. She reminded everyone that people were sick and dying and needed help. With O'Rourke they cleared out hotels and boardinghouses so they could take care of the sick. Molly and her girls were said to be tireless workers, even going up to the shacks and cabins of ill men to offer what care they could. It is said that she was so busy that she went long periods of time without eating or changing her clothes. Some of this story is true, but the details have been spun as the story was passed down.

The epidemic waned, but the hard work and poor eating habits affected her. The once robust Molly had lost weight and was sickly. She didn't have her usual energy. By October of the next year, Molly had fevers and a cough. She tried to keep her humor up, but her friends could tell that she was seriously ill. By the next month she was bedridden. The doctor confirmed that she had tuberculosis. Many of the town women (ladies who in most western towns would hardly say hello to a woman of Molly's profession) stayed by her bedside to comfort her. She was a fallen woman, but she was a friend. O'Rourke visited often, too. Molly continued to get worse. On January 17, 1888, Molly B'Dam, Maggie Hall, was dead.

In honor of her life, every curtain was closed, every blind was drawn, and the doors of the gambling parlors and drinking establishments were closed. Even the mines and sluice boxes closed. Thousands of people came to pay their respects to the tall, perky Irish lady. The stone marker on her grave reads:

Sacred
To the Memory of
Maggie Hall
Molly-B-Dam
Died At Murray
Jan. 17, 1888
Age 35 Years

She was really just thirty-four, so the inscription is off a year. For those interested, every August, Murray, Idaho, hosts an annual city celebration called the "Molly B'Dam Gold Rush Days." (Google Molly B'Dam Gold Rush Days for more information.) ⊷

CHAPTER ELEVEN

ANNIE GROVES

He Gave Her Syphilis, so She Shot but Missed

Nineteen-year-old Annie Groves, prostitute, was a long way from Kansas. The pistol felt heavy but reassuring in her sweating hand. She was still weak from her illness but determined that the man who infected her would pay.

She saw her sallow reflection in the window at Smizer's Saloon and looked at her bottom lip. It had been pretty, one of her best features. Now it swelled out like an infected blister, like the jutting jaw on a spawning trout. A bolt of anger and shame surged through her body. She fully intended to murder James E. Passwater. She hoped he would die a painful death. It was October 1907, and Wyoming evenings were getting crisp. Few shoppers were out this late. It was empty at the back of the saloon where she stood. Passwater, her ex-lover, was at the table, drinking and playing cards. Without hesitation, Annie held up her pistol, perhaps resting the bore on the window pane to steady the shaking. Aiming at James' head, the man who had caused all her troubles, she squeezed the trigger and hoped to watch him expire.

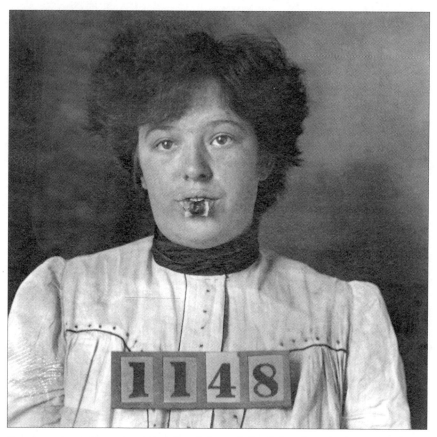

Prostitute Annie Groves contracted syphilis and decided to shoot the man who infected her. She was sentenced to a year in prison. She was Wyoming inmate #1148.

COURTESY OF WYOMING STATE ARCHIVES, DEPARTMENT OF STATE PARKS AND CULTURAL RESOURCES.

She wasn't an experienced markswoman. Annie missed her man, but she murdered his Stetson hat. At the same time, Annie managed to put a nasty hole in the shoulder of a certain Louis Peterson, who happened to be in the wrong place at the wrong time. A hat, after all, does little to stop a .45-caliber bullet. Peterson's wound was not fatal, but it didn't make his day pleasant. It also ruined his poker game. James wasn't about to stick around with a crazy woman waving a handgun at him, even if she was his former lover and partner in the venal trade. Making sure that Peterson was taken care of, James Passwater did what any sensible man in Wyoming would have done when given his options. Looking carefully to make sure he wasn't in the line of fire, he crossed the street and ran to the nearest police station like a scared jackrabbit. He hastily swore out an attempted murder complaint before S. E. Ferree, Justice of the Peace, Encampment, Wyoming. James said that Annie Groves "Willfully and maliciously perpetrated an assault and battery upon him . . . intending to kill him by shooting him with a gun." His hat was excellent proof, if the wound in Peterson wasn't enough. The woman had lost her senses.

Constable J. J. Wirth arrested Annie and brought her back to the jail. There wasn't a lot going on, so Justice Ferree conducted Annie's hearing that evening. He asked her if she had a lawyer. He discovered that the frightened woman was nearly destitute and had not been able to work. The court appointed her a public defender. Her counsel, a man named McMicken, wasted little time on his duties. Perhaps he needed to get home and tuck in his kids; maybe he thought the case was open and shut. She was a prostitute, after all, and she had tried to kill James Passwater. There wasn't much he could do. His advice to Annie was simple, "Throw yourself on the mercy of the court." Following his advice, Annie pleaded guilty.

Annie was taken by Sheriff Horton to the Carbon County jail where she would be tried before the Third Judicial District Court. It felt like she had lived forever, even if she was only nineteen years old. She thought of her childhood in Kansas, her loving parents who had taught her right from wrong. They had been Methodists. Her life had spun out of control, and now she was facing serious jail time for attempted murder. She had not told them her real name. Her parents would never find out the shame she had brought upon herself. She was what she was.

Annie had come to Encampment because it was a boomtown. Copper mines were the draw, and there was plenty of business for a girl in her trade. She was married to a man named E. J. Groves, who she hoped might be of some help. As a husband he left a lot to be desired, and the relationship turned bad. She had been a successful prostitute and soon became associated with James Passwater, who, at least for a while, had been more than a client. Passwater had a good job as the manager of the telephone network. Not one to stay home nights reading the Lake poets, Passwater was a lady's man. It seemed, at least, that he had been with one lady of the evening too many.

A Night with Venus
Was a Lifetime with Mercury

Any venereal disease was a serious problem. Treatments were crude and dangerous—or they did nothing at all. The most serious treatment, and the one that gave the victim a chance of being cured, was mercury. Mercury, though, was not without risks. The old cliché *"A night with Venus meant a lifetime with Mercury"* was too often painfully true.

Mercury has been used to treat venereal disease for nearly 3,000 years. In the fourth century B.C., medical practitioners in India used mercury topically. Chinese physicians of the day followed suit. In the early fifteenth century, Barbarossa, a Turkish admiral, gave his venereally-infected sailors a mercury pill for its healing effects. Even in early America, mercury was an important part of a doctor's medical bag. Look no further than the medicine chest the Lewis and Clark Expedition carried in 1804. Venereal disease was a frequent complaint among the Corps of Discovery, as was the treatment. The cure wasn't as bad as the disease, but it was very unpleasant. Mercury can cause severe itching and burning, as well as rashes and shedding of skin. Overexposure leads to loss of hair, teeth, fingernails, and toenails. Continued exposure causes tremors, weakness, and paralysis.

By the nineteenth century, a doctor might prescribe breathing vapors of mercury. On other occasions, he might smear mercury over the patient's body and then cover him with a blanket in a hot room or a sweat lodge. Or he might prescribe a calomel pill, which is mercury chloride in a dense white or yellow solid formed into a tablet. If a patient had chancres, pox, or rash, mercury was used topically. Less pleasant would be a small amount of mercury injected into the private parts. For men, a long syringe would be inserted up the urethra.

Treatment did come at a price. Mercury is not only toxic to syphilis and gonorrhea, it is poisonous to the patient. The trick was to kill the infection without killing the person. Many were killed by the cure. A small topical application was sometimes effective and offered the least risk. Otherwise, when sores in the mouth developed, if gums bled, or teeth fell out, treatment was stopped. At this point, the patient hoped the infection was killed. If the treatment went too far, kidney or heart failure was common.

Passwater had passed on a particularly virulent case of syphilis to Annie Groves, which had quickly become systemic. She had broken out in large pox-like sores and suffered other flu-like symptoms that typically accompany such a case. The raw sores were painful, but she thought she could live with them because she hoped they would pass. Later, however, a huge open sore formed on her lower lip, and it marred her looks. No one wanted a girl who was obviously infected; besides, she was too sick to pursue her vocation. She had sunk pretty low. She was well educated for her day, having graduated from the ninth grade. She was too knowledgeable to believe in the all-too-common folk remedies that still had a wide circulation among prostitutes. She knew the only way to be cured, if she were lucky, was by a doctor, and that would involve mercury treatment. She had seen the doctor and had taken some treatments, but the bills had mounted up. She sent note after note to James, asking him to help her with the medical bills—the least he could do was visit her. It was his fault, after all. He knew he had the disease, and he had been with her. She felt he owed her something. She pleaded again for him to help her with her medical bills. He ignored her. Annie claimed at one point that he got so tired of her nagging that he beat her. After the beating and his indifference concerning her condition, she decided to get even. With the terror of her disease, her lip likely ruined, her money gone, the best alternative was to blow his head off.

After two days in the Carbon County jail, Annie Groves was brought before the judge. She stood by herself, hoping for the best. The prosecuting attorney charged her with a felony for attempted murder against James Passwater with a loaded handgun. The jury didn't wait long to deliberate on the merits of the case. They found Groves guilty. The judge sentenced her to one year of hard labor in the state prison. That evening she was taken to the state penitentiary in Rawlins to serve her sentence.

In the meantime, James Passwater quit his high-paying job and took off for parts unknown. Apparently, he had a better job offer somewhere . . . anywhere. He didn't leave a forwarding address. Many felt he was being prudent in case Annie was released early. He must have felt that he had dodged a bullet once, but that he might not again when she got out of jail.

As an inmate, Annie was agreeable. One year for attempted murder was a light sentence. Meanwhile, her estranged husband, E. J. Groves, was

Prison doors were designed to resist escape, but their appearance also instilled a sense of resignation among inmates. COURTESY LIBRARY OF CONGRESS.

working on her release at the state level. Considering his past performance as a husband, this seemed like a Herculean task. He talked to Governor Brooks. Despite the jury's verdict, public opinion was on Annie's side, so it was easy for the governor to send a letter to the Board of Pardons. In less than five months, Annie was a free woman. Before she was released, E. J. Groves headed east to farming country. It's rumored that Annie followed him, presumably in gratitude.

CHAPTER TWELVE

SADIE ORCHARD

It's Always Been about the Money

S adie Orchard dreamed of being a prosperous Victorian woman with a proper Victorian life and a proper Victorian garden. She studied British magazines and knew how to put up her hair and dress like a stylish English woman of fashion. Sadie's family had been poor. She watched her mother die when she was thirteen. Her mother had worked herself to death eking out a hand-to-mouth existence while bearing at least ten children. In spite of their poverty, Sadie's parents wanted the best for her. It was a sacrifice, but her parents saw that she was educated. She could read rather well, she could write, and she could do her sums. Sadie came west in her twenties, seeking a better life. She never found Victorian gentility, but she learned how to be a proper whore and a successful madam. She was well appreciated by the rowdy men who frequented her professionally—as well as the city fathers whose favors she cultivated. And while Sadie might not have been invited to high tea with the local socialites, for a whore, she did not appear to suffer social ostracism. She took an active role in fundraising and building a church. She was a voice in civic affairs. She had candy for young children, and

Born Sarah Jane Creech into an impoverished Iowa farm family, Sadie Orchard headed west at twenty-five to find her fortune. Her business acumen led to a successful life as a madam, hotelier, and owner of a stagecoach line.
COURTESY OF PALACE OF THE GOVERNORS PHOTO ARCHIVES (NMHM/DCA).

she kept animals. Unlike most working girls, she dressed like a respectable woman and enjoyed long rides on her horse—British sidesaddle, of course.

During the horrific outbreak of the influenza virus in 1918, a global pandemic that killed more than 50 million people, she was a tireless worker with little regard for her own health. Even in her small town of Hillsboro, New Mexico, nearly two out of four residents had symptoms from the devastating flu epidemic that was sweeping the United States. She nursed the ill, changed bedpans, fed the weak, washed clothes, and comforted the sick and dying. It was said that when graves could not be dug fast enough, she reportedly helped dig graves and bury the dead. Her heart went out to ill children. When a child died, she supposedly used her fancy clothing to line the casket.

Sadie was a bold woman. Kindhearted, probably, but she'd seen too much life to completely trust the milk of human kindness. Being a prostitute was a hazardous business. There was always the threat of physical violence from an angry or deranged client. Then there were the nice men who turned angry after they started to drink. Most women in her profession had some sort of a revolver or a knife hidden on their person or stashed nearby. To complicate matters further, it wasn't only clients who posed a threat. A working girl also faced a threat from fellow bawdy girls or zealous madams.

Sadie's world was precarious. It's evident that she carried and knew how to use firearms. There is no record of her having a weapon "issue" with a client, however. The local paper would have written it up if she had. However, her personal life and weapons are another story. When her marriage to James Orchard turned sour, she lost some of her better judgment and was a bit too trigger-happy. Because of a domestic squabble, she was charged with discharging a weapon in city limits. She claimed that she was assaulted and was protecting herself. Later that summer, after a series of stormy spats with her husband, an argument over a carriage pushed her anger over the edge. The heated shouting match nearly turned deadly. Furious, Sadie drew her pistol and fired; the bullet hit rather near her husband's feet. Sadie claimed that she was only trying to scare him, not hit him. Then she told investigating officers that it was an accidental discharge. James didn't come to her defense. The fur continued to fly as the pair fought over other personal and business matters. The following winter, Sadie was charged with threatening to use deadly force. The local paper, *The Advocate*, noted all the delicious details for its curious readers. By 1901, the marriage ended bitterly in divorce. The feisty Sadie, angry with her ex-husband, reportedly ran James off one final time. To make her point, she peppered him with a double dose of birdshot from her 12-gauge shotgun.

Other than the tempestuous times when her marriage was breaking up, Sadie kept out of the limelight, preferring a low profile. She fostered relationships with important men in leadership positions because she knew such relationships were good for her business and could help protect her interests. She paid her city fines and license fees without incident and kept a tight lid on the women who worked for her. She would not allow them to be unruly or boisterous. A prostitute who was loud, drew attention to herself, or was publicly lewd would soon be asked to leave town, often forcibly. Sadie dressed modestly and conservatively and asked her girls to do likewise, which drew less public attention to their trade. Sadie shunned gaudy, revealing clothes so common among women of her profession. She wore long dark skirts and dresses and petticoats, often with white blouses that buttoned at the collar. She wore dark button-up shoes and stylish hats. Her hair was stacked on her head as was the fashion, especially for a stylish British lady of manners, just the sort she so admired. During her day, many prostitutes wore their hair loose. Wild, free-flowing hair was one of the less-subtle ways a prostitute distinguished herself from decent women. A "good" woman wore a cap or hat or her hair put up. The only time she would "let her hair down" was in her home. Sadie felt that if a working girl was out of sight, it was almost as if she wasn't there. Sadie recognized, too, that there was a social code of behavior, and she did not buck it. Houses that allowed the girls to smoke and drink in public or make lewd comments to men or women passing by were more likely to be raided and were the targets for the moral purity movements in a town.

Western New Mexico was a long way from the Kansas of Sadie's youth. Perhaps because of her careful manners and natural elegance, many of her friends and clients thought she was from England, which pleased her. There is even a legend that before her marriage broke up, she and James went to England for a visit to her "ancestral" home. Some of the lore that surrounds her life even suggests that she got rid of James in England and came back alone. Of course, none of this is true.

Sarah Jane Creech was born in Mills County, Iowa, in 1860 on a farm near the town of Tabor. (Her gravestone says she was born in 1862. This was a mistake, according to the Mills County Census.) Her nickname was Sadie. She was taught how to read and write and do arithmetic; whether she attended a school or learned from her parents is an open question. After her mother died, her father took the grieving family to Kansas. We know her family was poor, but information about her teenage years is very sparse. She helped her family, but there was barely enough to eat. Several of her siblings were farmed out to relatives. Young Sadie knew that she needed to make her way in the world as a young teenager. By 1885, she was headed west to Kingston, New Mexico, to seek her fortune. She wanted to see new places and travel. We can assume that she had already been indoctrinated into the world's oldest profession by the time she was fifteen. How she entered the profession remains a mystery. But like most women of that time, it was the only way she could support herself. A ticket out West was expensive, and she must have worked to have earned the money. She probably heard talk about how lucrative a boomtown might be, and she wanted to try her luck.

In 1885, the West was still wild. Just before she moved, Apache Indian attacks were a real danger for travelers. The forts were understaffed, and outlying ranches and prospectors who trespassed on traditional home-lands could be victims of raids. Even after the tribes were corralled on reservations, young bucks and disillusioned warriors who wanted the old ways back left the reservations and went on the warpath. The Apache war-rior was not noted for his kindness, leaving death and destruction in his wake. Victorio, Nana, and Geronimo ranged through Sadie's part of the Southwest. She had an unnatural fear of an Indian attack. She was safe enough in town, but the stories of Apache retribution terrified her.

In 1885, Kingston was a prosperous boomtown. Miners were flocking like geese to the Black Range to seek their fortunes. They were willing to risk marauding Apaches and harsh climatic extremes. Living conditions in the field were primitive at best, and the food was monotonous—if not

Madam Etta Clark:
An Abusive Madam

A bawdy girl lived in fear of physical violence, an unfortunate aspect of her trade. Worse, because she was a prostitute, a fallen woman, law enforcement was frequently indifferent. Sometimes her customers doled out the abuse. But it might also come from fellow prostitutes or a madam. Some madams were physically abusive, even killing a boarder or two. Madams held a considerable amount of control over their women, and many sheriffs left it up to them to police their ranks as they saw fit.

Etta Clark was a comely woman and popular with men. She was five feet tall and well proportioned. She was skilled at flattering and pleasing her clients, especially the wealthy ones, and she expected nothing less from her girls. She also had a wicked temper and was said to be meaner than a rattlesnake. With a potty mouth that would please a drill sergeant, she ran a strict house. In the border town of El Paso, Texas, there was money to be made, and Etta wanted as much as she could get.

The harder her girls worked, the more she made. She was so greedy, she would openly steal from her girls. Like most madams, she billed her bawdy girls for their laundry, food, rent, and sick time. She also required them to wear nice clothes, for which she charged inflated prices. If a prostitute got sick or business slowed, it was easy for her to get into more debt than she could ever pay off. Etta was happy to carry the deficit because it gave her more control. When a woman worked in a brothel, many madams felt they owned all the whore's clothes and personal possessions. If a prostitute fell too far in debt or was no longer making enough money for the house, an unscrupulous madam could throw a girl out on the street and keep her possessions.

On one occasion, Etta became so angry with some of her employees, she beat them up and threw them out on the street. In 1882, several of her employees sued her to get back their possessions. Her malicious reputation had preceded her to court. There were eight lawsuits in all. The madam was forced to make reparations to each of the working girls, paying back the market value of what she had taken.

lousy. It goes without saying that mining was physically brutal with few breaks during the day. Most men worked from daylight until dark. It was a dangerous life. When they came to town, it was to replenish supplies and blow off steam. Drinking, gambling, and women were a short respite from the realities and frustrations of their work. In spite of a splitting hangover, empty pockets from last night's faro table, or the haunting fear of a bad disease from the girl last night, a new day's optimism seemed to erupt in a miner—the next swing of a pick or the next shovel of dirt might be the one that made him rich.

Kingston was a town where an enterprising woman could make a lot of dollars. A miner named Jack Sheddon had discovered a rich vein of silver in 1882. His mine, the Solitaire, was one of the most famous in the Southwest. At its peak, the population of Kingston was greater than 7,000, mostly men. Kingston was known as the one of the wildest, most sinful towns in the Southwest. Saturday nights the town was so jammed with miners looking for a good time that it was almost impossible to move through the crowds. Even with its wide streets, the town was so packed it was said to take over an hour to go from one end of town to the other. Besides gambling parlors, twenty-two saloons, and several bawdy houses, there was an opera house, hotels, fourteen general stores, three newspapers, restaurants, shops, and theatres. The fame of this town drew Grover Cleveland, Mark Twain, Butch Cassidy, and the Sundance Kid, among others. The miners hoped to get rich (more than $7 million worth of silver was taken from the Black Range in the 1880s and 1890s).

This was just what Sadie was looking for, a lot of love-starved men away from home with money to burn. Legend has her opening up a prosperous bawdy house on the "wicked" Virtue Avenue as soon as she arrived, but this doesn't seem quite accurate. Sadie had saved enough money to make the trip west and to tide her over, but she certainly didn't have enough capital to start her own business in a new town—especially with the inflated prices one had to pay in a boomtown. Instead, she probably went to work for another house and saved her money. We do know that before a year was out, she was one of the most popular girls on the line—establishing a reputation for being charming, witty, and congenial, among other talents. She appears to have earned enough money to start her own house, be it ever so humble. Unlike most girls who spent their money on clothes and vices of choice, Sadie had a plan and wanted a bigger piece of the action.

Before long, Sadie considered moving nine miles away to another thriving town called Hillsboro. It would be a prudent move. In 1886, she took her nest egg, her girls, and perhaps some investors, and she moved. It was a smaller town, but there were plenty of customers. Maybe establishing a business in Hillsboro was less expensive. Being in a smaller town made her feel a little more vulnerable to Apache attacks (even into the 1890s there were still isolated raids on miners and ranchers), but business was business. Her bawdy house was an instant success, and Sadie made excellent money. She was up front with her clients and demanded that her girls were likewise. There was no tawdry or cheap behavior. Nor would she keep a girl who took advantage of or stole from a customer. She recognized that she was running a business for the long term, not just a string of one-night stands. It was good business to be fair and keep repeat customers. Sadie was also politically savvy. As rowdy towns started to settle down and respectable women moved in, town councils tended to start limiting houses of prostitution. As a result of Sadie's commonsense approach, her business was able to ride out many of the purges imposed by religious leaders and women's groups on the town's vices. Furthermore, in the back of Sadie's mind was the hope of making a lot of money and giving up prostitution. She wanted to be in business and invest in other business interests. Perhaps she'd keep the whorehouse as a sideline but hire someone else to run it and distance herself from her old line of work. It had always been her dream to become a respected Victorian woman, and prostitution made that difficult. Another part of her plan was to get married, a major step in establishing respectability. It's hard to know if her plan to marry was sincere or a business strategy, but she conveniently fell in love with James W. Orchard, a well-heeled businessman. The lovebirds were married in July 1895. It appears that after her nuptials, she left her profession as a madam and a prostitute, but it's not certain if she sold, leased, or subcontracted her brothel.

James owned the Orchard-Matthewson Stage Line. She joined the business with her husband. She enjoyed being in a legitimate enterprise

Mrs. Sadie Orchard in front of the Ocean Grove Hotel.

PHOTOGRAPH BY GEORGE T. MILLER, COURTESY PALACE OF THE GOVERNORS PHOTO ARCHIVES
(NMHM/DCA), #076560.

and bragged that their newest coach carried nine passengers and was pulled
by eighteen horses. The stage business' bottom line depended on whether
or not they got the local mail contract, but they planned to expand. Her
future looked promising. Whether Sadie invested some of her own money
in the business is not known, but she did put her soul into making it a
success. A clever businesswoman, she ran much of the day-to-day business operations. It was costly to keep the horses, coach, and tack in repair,
so they worked on growing their customer base. The mail contract was
frequently up for bid, so they had to stay competitive. Legend has it that
Sadie was an occasional driver when the regular driver or her husband
could not make the five-hour run to Lake Valley and back. She might
have driven a few times, and Sadie was probably capable and willing to
do this if she had to, but most of the stories of her driving are folklore.
This was the 1890s, and many men—no matter how skilled a driver Sadie
was, no matter how acquainted she was with livestock—would not have

had confidence in a female coachman. More important, Sadie was trying to be a lady, and respectable ladies didn't drive stagecoaches. We have to remember that while she loved horses, she rode sidesaddle.

In 1896, the couple expanded their business concerns. James gave Sadie a corner lot where he built a hotel for her. There were six rooms. Sadie set them up in proper Victorian fashion and called her new place Ocean Grove. Knowing how important good food was, Sadie hired the best cook in town, Tom Ying, stealing him from her competition by offering him a better wage. She was fair with Ying, and the fact that he stayed with her for many, many years gives us an idea about how well she treated him and her other employees. She ran a clean hotel and was very busy. It was often booked up for weeks at a time. Because the Ocean Grove was so successful under her management, the couple opened up another hotel, called the Orchard. It, too, thrived under her care.

Unfortunately, the Orchards' relationship did not prosper as well as their businesses. By 1900, their relationship was strained. Sadie, who made it a rule to stay out of the public eye, had loud public arguments with James. It must have made her angry to see her personal life reported in the local paper. She was mad at James and at herself. She knew that every time the paper reported a shooting incident, her respectability sank. After the divorce, she kept the Ocean and the Orchard. She continued to run the Ocean, which was a moneymaker, especially with Tom Ying's cooking. She remodeled the Orchard and turned it into a low-profile brothel, which stayed in business for another thirty years. By the 1930s, she was still running both businesses, and Tom Ying was still cooking for her (they charged only three cents for a cup of strong, black coffee). She went to church regularly and was active in civic affairs. A famous icon from the Old West, in spite of her profession, she was liked. Her true story is more interesting, indeed, than many of the exaggerated legends about her. Sadie had seen the frontier West and been a part of it. She had moved into the wild Southwest when everyone carried a gun and Apaches still raided across their traditional homeland. She wanted respect, which she partly earned, but she never became a Victorian lady, although she did read British poetry. She achieved some measure of economic prosperity, but too late to help her family.

In the last few years of her life, Sadie suffered from paralysis of the nervous system, which was a complication of syphilis. At the ripe age of eighty-three, on April 3, 1943, Sadie, the old pioneer, passed to her reward, hopefully a Victorian reward, and was buried at Truth or Consequences, New Mexico, formerly known as Hot Springs. As writer Erna Fergusson so aptly suggested, "For a bad woman, Sadie was one of the best." ⊶

CHAPTER THIRTEEN

MOLLIE JOHNSON
Sassy Queen of the Blondes

Mollie Johnson was the self-proclaimed "Queen of the Blondes." More important, Madam Mollie was also the undisputed master of whorehouse public relations. She could turn a simple spat among her ladies into a prosperous media circus. For Mollie, any press was good press because exposure with the correct spin was good for business. While she was in a dirty profession, she had the timing of a modern-day ad executive and the savage instincts of a Wall Street banker. After Dora DuFran, Mollie Johnson was the second most successful madam on the Northern Plains. Both women based their businesses in Deadwood, in the Black Hills. Strangely enough, Mollie and Dora managed to become good friends, which was unusual among competing madams with competing houses. Usually, such a situation would've led to bitter rivalry. In this case, however, each madam stuck to her strengths, which let them coexist. Dora was concerned about good service and employee relationships. Mollie was concerned about branding, advertising, and volume.

Dora didn't mind flying under the social radar, letting her business take its natural course as quietly as she could. Mollie, on the other hand, intentionally broke the social sound barrier, keeping her life, her girls' lives, or her house continually in the public eye—no matter how petty or foolish. It didn't matter what folks were saying as long it was about her or her business. Besides good public relations, Mollie tried to set her house apart from the competition. For example, all her girls had blonde hair (even if it was out of a bleach bottle). It was her way of branding, her bawdy trademark, setting her bad girls apart. To punctuate this, she, of course, called herself the Queen of the Blondes. If it was a slow week, Mollie might stir things up. Along with her girls, Ida Clark, Jennie Duchesneau, and Ida Cheplan, the shady ladies would dress up in their fanciest clothes, make their hair perfect, and take special care with their makeup. It was time to employ one of her favorite gimmicks, so her house would be sure to pick up a few lines in the next edition of the paper and revitalize the business with the local clientele. Mollie hired a fancy carriage for $10 an hour. She had the coachman drive her bevy of strumpets around the city in grand fashion. The girls were extra friendly. They waved to everyone while showing off their frilly clothing, their painted-bawdy beauty, and their current availability. They assumed an air of cathouse false-maiden modesty as they mildly flirted with men on the sidewalks. Mollie wanted everyone to see how attractive and cuddly her girls were. Because they were out in public, the prairie nymphs were especially polite and social, nothing lewd or indiscreet. Mollie wanted the men in Deadwood to know that the Queen of the Blondes had the best.

In the spirit of public relations and good business, Mollie liked to throw big dances at the Fireman's Hall. In the West, dancing with a pretty woman, especially in Deadwood where men outnumbered women, could be costly. Men would go to a dance hall (which could be a brothel, too) and pay by the dance. Buying a number of watered-down drinks was also part of the dance ticket. Mollie's dances, however, were free, and men came for miles just to see, let alone dance with, a pretty girl. Of course, the purpose of this fandango wasn't simply goodwill or public high-mindedness. It was advertising, and it worked. The girls would be booked up afterward.

While Mollie was a brazen businesswoman, she had a lesser-known vulnerable side. She would help poor settlers or stake a hungry man to a dinner. When Miss Jennie Phillips, one of Mollie's girls, died, Mollie was distraught. The two were close, and Mollie thought of Jennie as a surrogate

By the 1890s, Deadwood was a prosperous town of about 3,500 with all the amenities—and vices—of much larger metropolises. COURTESY LIBRARY OF CONGRESS.

daughter as well as a good friend. Poor Jennie suffered from a short illness and suddenly passed on. The cause of her death was a mystery, although some of Jennie's friends speculated that she got an infection from a cat bite. (Jennie loved cats. Previously she tried to pet a feral cat in the alley. It wasn't friendly and savagely bit her, driving his teeth through her thumb.) In her grief Mollie saw that Jennie had the finest casket and put her body in the parlor of her brothel. The burial would be the next day. According to the *Black Hills Daily Times*, "The Madam who referred to the dead as 'my little girl' bowed in sorrow that was evidently genuine." In the parlor, the pictures were turned backwards and black cloth draped the doors and windows. That evening a tragedy occurred that was all too common in a frontier town. A fire started in the bakery, which quickly blazed out of control and consumed most of the town. Molly wasn't worried about saving her important possessions, which she could have done. Her only interest was saving Jennie's body. By the time the casket was removed, the fire was in the roof of her building, and in minutes the house had burned to the ground. The fire damage cost a little over $4,000. Mollie appeared nonplussed. The next morning an expensive hearse took Jennie Phillips' body to the cemetery. She was buried with as much pomp as Mollie could muster. Fires were common, and this would not be the last fire that threatened Mollie's place of business or Deadwood. In fact, one afternoon after she had rebuilt her place, a girl put wood that was too dry behind the stove, and the wall caught on fire. Fortunately, someone noticed, and several buckets of water extinguished the flames.

Newspaper reporters as well as the *Black Hills Daily Times* appeared to be marionettes in Mollie's bordello puppet show. Prostitutes were not the most stable human beings, especially in the closed confines of a brothel, and they often fought with one another, occasionally causing serious injury. Newspapers liked to capitalize on such skirmishes, sometimes reporting a blow-by-blow account over a number of editions. The *Black Hills Daily Times* was no exception. Indeed, the paper at one point had a fixation on Mollie and her girls, reporting at length on every trivial dispute. Perhaps there were slow news days in the Gulch. At first it seems inconsequential, but when you look at it from a business point of view, the whorehouse couldn't buy better advertisement. It was more than coincidental. Maybe it was a lazy or a bored reporter, or perhaps a reporter who was interested in Mollie's favors. Someone who was willing to trade news space for services rendered. We don't know, of course, but it is a possibility. A reporter trying to get a rise out of the local prostitutes to make some bylines—even if he had a little help.

Newspapers in the 1870s were neither unbiased nor objective. Papers and individual reporters often had political and personal axes to grind, and they weren't subtle about it. Journalist ethics, as we know them today, at least theoretically, were not a part of a newsman's job description. As any historian or research buff knows, referencing a nineteenth-century reporter or a newspaper text does not give one an objective view of history. Nor is it an accurate accounting of the facts. It's an important source of information, but it's not definitive. Consider the tone of this newspaper piece in the *Evening Call* about a man who got drunk and was rolled in the red light district. Notice how the writer editorializes a so-called news piece:

Jack M., who is well known in this city, got touched for his money in Deadwood last night down on Green Street . . . . He is an old timer in this community and everyone who knows him will be surprised at the easy manner in which he was fleeced. He lost $100 and up to this date is still out the money. This should satisfy Jack with the sinful city and teach him to come to Lead where there is no danger.

In several *Black Hills Daily Times* pieces, we can see that the reporter was almost baiting the local bawds, trying to stir up one house against another. If fur flew, he would have an easy article to write—and the readership would love it. In one such piece, Mollie was pitted in the press against three prostitutes from another house. The reporter wrote that a trio of trollops had been arrested for "selling hooch without a license." The reporter implied that the information used to arrest the ladies in question was cleverly slipped to law enforcement from none other than Madam Mollie Johnson, herself, the Queen of the Blondes. Further, the reporter wrote that Mrs. Johnson had rolled over on these poor working girls because she, Mollie, felt that they were getting a little bit uppity, and they needed to be punished; Mollie set up the "corralling of her lascivious sisters" to teach them a lesson.

To keep her name in the public eye, and to ease the tension among the three women who were incarcerated, Mollie eagerly sent a short note to the *Times*, which it promptly published. "I know nothing of the ladies referred to. I am the least one to do injury to these ladies, or as you say, my sisters in sin." All press was good press for this business, and Mollie turned it to her advantage. It was free advertising. If the paper slacked off and reported on other things, Mollie, according to legend, did something newsworthy. One legend has her riding her horse into a saloon, stopping in front the bar, and ordering a drink. (The saloon must have had very large, tall doors, or she had a very short horse. Apparently, her mount was not afraid of batwing doors, either.) On other occasions, folks said, when Mollie was feeling lazy, she'd stop at the hitching post and have some lucky loafer get her a drink.

Baseball was popular in the West, and there was no law that said a bunch of professional ladies couldn't be fans. Mollie and her girls loved the game. Rooting for a favorite team was a delightful pastime, but it was thirsty work. One summer evening, Mollie and the girls got a bit tipsy after a few innings. As the story is told, when the ballgame was over, the drunken bawds decided to race their buggies across the plains. When you are seriously over the limit, somehow knowing who among your ranks was the fastest buggy driver seemed very important, even if racing across the rugged prairie might not be the better part of valor. The ground was rough and dangerous, but the girls were too far under to notice or care. At speeds no sober driver would travel, the inexperienced painted ladies whipped their buggy-chariots faster than any angel might fear to tread. One girl hit a bump and lost control of her buggy. She might have had several passengers, depending on who told the story. It would have added to the merriment. The specifics of the adventure get a little foggy in the telling because the men who were watching were drinking bourbon or gin or rotgut, and no one's mind was clear.

One unfortunate racer, probably too drunk to appreciate the gravity of her situation, flew head over heels through the air like a broken toy until she planted herself in the dry prairie, her buggy exploding into pieces about her. A couple of men who had been watching the fun stumbled to the rescue of the wounded tart, loading the injured woman into the other racing buggy, which had also tipped. The men righted the cart and promptly drove her off to get medical care in Deadwood. All the other men followed them on their horses. Focusing on the injured girl, and likely seeing double as it was, they left Mollie and the remaining girls stranded on the prairie. The *Times*, not missing a chance to take a humorous poke, reported, "Madam [Mollie] and the other golden-haired sirens [were left] afoot upon the boundless prairie. In the meanwhile night dropped her sable curtain down and pinned it with a star, and our three heroines like Hagar were left crying in the wilderness." Surely a madder-than-hell Mollie and her three sister sirens, sore-footed and hungover, didn't burn the red lantern that night.

Mollie was an iconoclast, but not an eccentric. Her movements seem too well calculated and planned. Being a prostitute meant that she broke with the conventional norms of polite society and was socially ostracized from normal life. Her profession and her peculiar behaviors would have pushed other fallen women over the edge, but Mollie knew how to bounce back. She flirted with the extreme edge of propriety, often stepping over, but always stepping back. She never allowed it to swallow her. She did, however, push her social envelope to the limit in 1878. Local gossip reports that she married a black man. A white woman, even a prostitute, did not socialize or allow a black man to visit her. If she did, she could be completely ostracized or run out of business. Some women were carried out of town on a rail after being tarred and feathered. For the black man, any sort of sexual liaison with a white woman could be a hanging offense. Such a relationship was rarely heard of, yet legend has Mollie taking the racial plunge.

Newspapers were not silent on the possible liaison. Allegedly, she married Lew Spencer, who was a singer and a comedian at the Bella Union Theater. He was referred to as "Dutch Nigger." We know little about the relationship, but the so-called marriage, if it actually took place, drew attention with surprisingly little effect on either of their careers. It's unusual that she was not run out of Deadwood. Perhaps it was such an outrageous accusation that few believed it actually occurred. We know that Lew left Deadwood after a short time, and the two likely never saw each other again. In retrospect, it might have been a fling. Lew went to Denver and soon found himself in serious trouble. In 1880 he was arrested for shooting his wife—not Mollie, but the woman he was legally married to. It appears Lew was, at the least, a bigamist or a cheating two-timer. Perhaps his legal wife had found out about his affair in Deadwood? Either way, there was a big blowout. He was thrown in jail for the killing. After doing some time, he was let out on good behavior and enjoyed a successful musical career.

Mollie Johnson's antics as a madam, her flash and glitter, are well documented. The rest of her life is sketchy. We know little about the real Mollie Johnson as a person. She used printed media like a skillful politician. She was the "shock rock" madam of her day, but she knew how to separate the woman from the stage act. So much about her persona was carefully orchestrated by this astute businesswoman. We know Mollie as the prostitute, we know her as the madam, and we know her as the keen and savvy professional woman. Her private life was private and was secreted away like a treasure in a locked jewelry box. Likely, she did this so she could retire in anonymity when her Deadwood gig had run its course.

We know from the Territorial Census in 1880 that she was born in Alabama and that she claimed to be twenty-seven years old. If she wasn't fibbing, that means she would have been born around 1852. Her family was probably of Irish descent since she was active in the Irish Famine Relief. Perhaps her family had been impoverished by the Civil War, or she was from a poor family or orphaned by the war. It's all speculation. Some reports have her becoming a soiled dove around the age of fifteen. She is said to have been widowed before coming to Deadwood. Who she was married to is a mystery. With a handful of women in Deadwood and thousands of lonely men, she picked an ideal location. In 1883, when the mining started to play out, Mollie Johnson, a wealthy woman, packed up and left. We have no idea where she went, because she was never heard from again. ⟞

CHAPTER FOURTEEN

JENNIE ROGERS

Queen of the
Colorado Underworld

Yes, Jennie Rogers, the Queen of the Colorado Underworld, had a temper. Even in her forties, Jennie was a beautiful woman with luscious jet-black hair. One of the most successful madams in Denver, she decided to make a surprise visit to her lover, a twenty-three-year-old man named John A. Wood. He went by the name of Jack. Jennie was excited to see him. A fellow horse lover, Jack had been impressed at how kindly and cleverly Jennie handled her horses. A friendship developed, and it appeared to be something special. She bought a small saloon so he could better himself, and he did. It was also a good investment. In spite of the difference in their ages, they fell in love like a couple of kids at a circus. Wanting to keep her business life removed from her personal life, she bought a drinking establishment in Salt Lake City and set Jack up to run it since he'd proven to be a good manager. She made frequent visits so they could be together.

Jennie was happy to have someone who really loved her, someone who was not after her money. So, on a whim, one day she bought a train ticket so she could see her true love, Jack. She burst into the love nest she had bought for the two of them, shouting "Surprise!" The surprise, however, was on her. She found her lover in a compromising way with another, younger woman. Embarrassed, crushed, and hurt, her heart was broken. Then her famous temper flared. There was only one thing she could do. She reached in her pocket and pulled out the trusty handgun she always carried and fired it at the only man she ever loved.

Jack tumbled over, and Jennie wondered if she had killed him. We assume the girl Jack was with ran off before Jennie shot her, too. The police quickly arrived, and Jennie uttered some of the most famous lines ever spoken by a woman scorned, "I shot him because I love him! Damn him!" Jennie's famous temper had gotten the better of her. She was arrested and put in jail for attempted murder. Fortunately, Jennie was a better businesswoman than she was a shooter. Jack was not severely wounded and told the police that the incident was his fault. Jennie was released, and she returned to Denver.

She didn't get over her two-timing lover, however, and fell into a deep depression. She hoped for a reconciliation. The madam who ran the second-best parlor house in Denver, the woman who had the prettiest whores, was like a schoolgirl with her first crush. She was wildly rich, but her money had not made her happy. She kept tabs on Jack, and the two finally reunited in 1889 and married on August 13. A few years later, Jack died suddenly. Again heartbroken, Jennie put "He Is Not Dead, He Is Sleeping" on his headstone. To try and overcome her grief, she dove into her business concerns.

Jennie Rogers, also professionally known as a Leeah J. Tehme and Leeah Fries, was born Leeah Calvington on July 4, 1843, in Allegheny, Pennsylvania, into abject poverty. Her father was a dirt farmer who had a hard time keeping food on the table. As a girl, Jennie helped all she could. When she got a little older, she would go into the city and sell produce. A tall, beautiful girl, she noticed that when she flirted with the men and boys, she sold more produce. She disliked farm life, and she hated being poor. She wished she had enough money to buy pretty things and stay at nice places. She had plans, and they didn't include staying on a two-bit dirt farm in Pennsylvania. A comely girl bursting out of her clothes, she

Jennie Rogers wanted more than a two-bit dirt farm in Pennsylvania. She headed west to seek her fortune. She quickly realized that prostitution only paid if you were a madam. She carved out her fortune and reputation in Denver where she called herself the Queen of the Underworld.

Fighting Madams: Was One Topless?

This is one of the most beloved tales in the West, and it's taller than it is true. In fact, there's probably nothing true about it at all, but no one seems to care.

Two of Denver's most beautiful madams fell for the same no-account drifter, a gambler named Cortez "Cort" Thompson. The irony is that either woman could have had just about any man east of the Rockies, but they both swooned for Cort, a card player who thought he was man enough for both women. Of course, there was only one way to settle the score: Kate Fulton and Mattie Silks would have to fight it out with six-shooters: the winner would take Cort.

The scene varies from one telling of the story to the next. Some say that perhaps they met at high noon on the banks of the Platte River outside of town to avoid local entanglements. Others recall it taking place on Holiday Street, not far from their respective houses in the shadiest part of town. Looking back, several old-timers who claimed to have watched the shootout say it took place in August. Others say April. It was also reported,

entertained marriage proposals, but she didn't want to be saddled to a section of land or a farm.

When an older, wealthy doctor asked for her hand, she surprised everyone and married him. He was often gone, so she was left alone. The living was easy, but she grew tired of an older man and wanted adventure. She took off with a fellow who traveled the rivers. It was exciting to see different cities, but she soon grew tired and left him also. She worked odd jobs, but mostly was a housekeeper.

A clever girl, she realized that single men wanted affection and conversation and were willing to pay for it. She decided this was something she could do and still keep her independence. She probably joined the professional life in St. Louis. She earned a good deal of money, so she prostituted herself but likely had other women working for her, too. Even at an early age, she had a good head for business. She apparently earned a nest egg of around $5,000 to $6,000. Since most brothels were poorly run, financial but not verified, that top-heavy Kate Fulton stepped upon the field of honor bare-breasted, the gentle breeze blowing her hair. If the beautiful and endowed Kate was indeed topless, it's no wonder so many men have forgotten the factual historical details. They were focused on . . . other things.

There was a lot of name calling at the start—both women could swear like track layers. Then a fight broke out, the buxom beauties scratching each other and pulling hair until they were pried apart. As in a formal duel, the seconds checked the Colt .45s to see that they were both loaded. This was not the first time the two had quarreled over Cort, but it would be the last because this was a fight to the death.

Determined to kill or be killed, the topless, stunning Kate and the gorgeous, exquisite Mattie strode toward each other. They both aimed and shot . . . and missed! Well, they missed each other. Cort had prudently moved back and out of the way. He was standing near the buggy in case he needed to make a prudent getaway or wanted to come forth and give himself to the woman who was left standing. Ironically, a wandering bullet from one of the pistols (we think it was Kate's weapon) hit Cort, and he went down. Then he got up. He had been grazed in the neck, an inconsequential flesh wound. Ironically, Cortez Thompson became Mattie's on-and-off lifetime lover. When she died in 1929, she was buried at his side.

solvency, let alone saving investment capital at an early age, speaks highly for her business skills. Seeking more adventure and wanting to make a profit, in 1880 Jennie turned west. A lot of lonely men on the frontier . . . it was exactly what she was looking for. Like so many women in her trade, she used a professional name. Usually a woman did this to preserve her dignity. And, if she were lucky enough to leave the bawdy business, she could use her real name. Probably the most important reason for a professional name was to preserve her family's dignity. No one wanted to have a daughter who was a whore.

The gold rush in Colorado, specifically Denver, drew her attention. We don't know if she sold her business in St. Louis or if her trip west was to purchase a second brothel. We know she liked Denver and decided to make the Mile-High City her home. There were other houses of prostitution, some doing very well, but Jennie felt she could do it better, and she would. For around $5,000 she bought a brothel. She decorated the rooms and

Mattie Silks: Queen of Denver's Red Light District

Mattie Silks entered the sisterhood when she was a teen. Always ambitious, she said, "I went in the sporting life for business reasons and for no other. It was always a way for a woman in those days to make money and I made it. I consider myself then, and do now, a business woman." This Denver working woman might have been one of the most successful madams in the American West, perhaps making $2 million before she died. She always insisted that she was never a prostitute, just a madam. She did honor the slogan, however, that hung on the wall of her brothel: "Men Taken in and Done For."

Mattie and a competitor and good friend, another Denver madam named Jennie Rogers, together were the reigning queens of prostitution in the Mile High City during the latter part of the nineteenth century. Rogers called herself the Queen of the Underworld. Mattie called herself the Queen of the Red Light District. In 1909, Mattie bought the elegant House of Mirrors after Jennie had left the Rocky Mountains for her health. After buying the elaborate brothel, Mattie added her own decorating touches. She retiled the front porch and had "M. Silks" written before the doors. She kept the famous house until 1919, when she sold it at a profit.

Mattie Silks and Jennie Rogers were excellent businesswomen who knew how to grease the political wheels. Each ran prosperous houses that made money. Both madams understood that it was critical to work with

Her profitable business allowed Mattie Silks (in hat and kimono) to indulge in her love for horses.
COURTESY DENVER PUBLIC LIBRARY, WESTERN HISTORY COLLECTION, #X-27055.

local government and not against it. For example, Mattie was able to purchase a liquor license in 1885, something rarely given to a brothel (most sold illegal alcohol).

Mattie started her first brothel in Springville, Illinois, around 1865 when she was about nineteen. Later, she moved to Kansas but pushed on when her house was shut down in a moral purge. Reportedly, she traveled with a group of bawdy girls going to the mining camps and cow towns. At some point, she allegedly married a tinhorn gambler named Silks, but there is no record of their marriage other than the fact that she took his name. The relationship soured, and Mattie moved to Denver, shy of her thirtieth birthday. She bought a house from a madam named Nellie French and never looked back.

In Denver, Mattie fell for a no-good gambler named Cortez "Cort" Thompson. Neither Mattie nor Jennie were good judges in men—both fell for gamblers or charlatans who leached off their wealth. Cort gambled poorly, yet Mattie loved him enough to keep him in gambling money and drinking money. Mattie was his meal ticket, and after repeated indiscretions, he crawled back to her, very sorry for his behavior . . . and then asked for money. The two married in 1884. He boasted that he was too proud to work. Over the span of their relationship, he might have bled Mattie for more than $100,000—a lot of money when the average man made $30 to $40 a month. Cort's losses at the gaming tables and his weakness for other women caused a lot of bickering. In 1891, they had a big fight and Mattie filed for divorce, but Cort talked her out of it. Then, in 1900, while they were at their ranch, Cort grew sick and died. He was buried with all the trimmings.

After Cort's death, Mattie hired a man named Jack Ready, also known as Handsome Jack. Jack helped her with her business affairs. Another gold digger, he cultivated her affections, though she was considerably older. Mattie fell for the younger man, who then managed to help himself to her money. The pair traveled in style, threw lavish parties, and spent money. Jack must have been disappointed when Mattie died. In 1929, the old madam, who had gained a considerable amount of weight, tripped and fell, breaking her hip. She was hospitalized but never recovered from her injury and died in her bed. She had only $4,000 left in her account.

(Continued on page 138)

Stupid with her affections, but a keen, successful madam, Mattie Silks prospered in a business that was usually brutal and cut-throat. With some lapses, she was mostly patient and understanding with the prostitutes she employed. Mattie prided herself on never hiring a girl who did not have experience. She never coerced or forced an employee to work for her or took advantage of someone's situation. It was a source of pride that she had bought many tickets home for many young women who looked at prostitution as a last choice.

Mattie Silks was a rival madam and a good friend of Jennie Rogers—although it was unusual to have two rival madams as friends. This image was taken of Mattie when she was forty years old.
COURTESY HISTORY COLORADO.

hired the prettiest, most seductive girls she could find. She also insisted that they live up to her code of behavior. She wanted them to act classy and uptown. She would not hire a girl who did not have good manners and some sort of education. Jennie brought in dressmakers and supervised as they made beautiful and fashionable clothes. It was expensive, but she wanted her house to be the best. Besides, she charged her girls for the extras she provided. She furnished the rooms with big brass beds, carved furniture, and expensive curtains.

Most brothels had windows that were nailed shut. This kept men from breaking in for a sneak visit. It also kept customers from leaving without paying their tabs. Jennie liked fresh air and thought the thick scent of tobacco smoke, perfume, and bodies was too much. She wanted every window to open; however, she did install iron bars so no one could break in or out. She stocked the finest cigars, wines, and liquors. Within several months, she reportedly earned back her investment. The move to Denver was a wise choice. The city was growing exponentially, and there was a lot of discretionary money. More important, a lot of single men roamed the town, men who enjoyed the sporting life. Denver's dens of sin, especially on Market Street where Jennie bought her brothel, were said to be so wicked and vice ridden that they rivaled San Francisco's Barbary Coast or New Orleans' Storyville. Furthermore, city government was corrupt. Bribery and intimidation were everyday business practices. Gambling dens, brothels, and prostitutes paid license fees, taxes, and fines; however, they were also expected to pay corrupt police and city officials under the table. Officials became rich. If the vice trades weren't a nuisance and stayed in their prescribed locations and paid fees and bribes, they were mostly ignored. Jennie Roger's parlor was high end and drew a lot of public officials, which gave her an added measure of protection from harassment.

With the profits from her business, Jennie invested in real estate, water shares, and other opportunities. While Denver vices managed to stay free of most legal entanglements, there were occasional officials who did not share the "liberal" view of how city government should be run. There were also outside influences, such as various women's movements that demanded something be done about the corruption. To capitulate to these special interest groups, city government would shake up the vice districts with showy arrests and added fines, but, overall, little changed. On one occasion, fifteen madams were arrested and fined for running disorderly houses, but all went back to work as soon as the officials pandered to the press to show how much they were doing to clean up the city.

In 1888, Jennie built a dream brothel that she called the House of Mirrors. As a point of interest, she used the name Leah J. Fries on the property deed. Her stock in trade was to have the best of everything and then charge extra for clients to enjoy it. She hired William Quayle, the noted architect. Her house had all the extras. It was three stories and had fifteen rooms, a wine cellar, servant's quarters, a large dining room, a spacious kitchen, a ballroom, and bedrooms. There were, of course, mirrors on the ceiling and walls, crystal chandeliers, and imported rugs. Her house was so lavish that local businessmen and politicians held meetings there. To the chagrin of a *Rocky Mountain News* reporter in 1890, "Each afternoon about three o'clock, the august lawmakers would retire to Jennie Roger's Palace of Joy on Market Street and there deport themselves in riotous fashion." Getting her house built was not a problem. Jennie had hosted a lot of important men, and she knew more than she should about personal and business matters and used it to her advantage. She had silent investors who were pleased to support her ventures to keep their secrets from seeing the light of day. She was not above subtle bribery and extortion to get what she wanted. She had cultivated important men to help her. She regularly slept with the Denver chief of police, or so she said, who became her lover and an instant connection to law enforcement if a bribe to cover some illegal activity didn't pan out. To get enough money to pay for her new brothel, it seems she blackmailed a man named Splevin for $17,000. She told him she had proof that he killed his first wife and that, unless he gave her the money, she would give the evidence to the chief of police. Reportedly, he gladly paid Jennie to keep quiet. The irony was that Jennie's evidence was manufactured, but Splevin didn't know it.

Jennie's business was doing well, but she was feeling worn down and tired. Her doctor had diagnosed her with Bright's disease (an ailment of the kidneys that causes back pain, hypertension, and stomach problems). He told her that she needed to leave Denver and go to a lower altitude. Prolonging her leaving until she was quite sick, she hired a manager for

Jennie Rogers displayed her wealth in the intricate carvings that embellished the exterior of her House of Mirrors, including buxom busts of women in the gable ends.

her business concerns and moved to Chicago. In the Windy City, she purchased another brothel after selling off some of her assets. Jennie needed something to keep her busy.

Lonely and vulnerable, the fifty-nine-year-old Jennie met a younger man named Archibald Fitzgerald, who was twenty-two years her junior. He was charming and polite, but as she'd discover, he was a gold digger. He gave her the attention that she craved. She was in love again, and the two married. Fitzgerald managed to swindle her out of a good piece of her fortune, but not before she discovered that he was still married to another woman, so she dumped him. Worried about her finances, her health weakened, and her situation became critical. She spent the last part of her life in a hospital and died at age sixty-nine on October 7, 1909.

Jennie Rogers was laid to rest in Denver next to her true love, John Wood. ⇥

CHAPTER FIFTEEN

MARY KATHERINE HORONY

Big Nose Kate, Doc Holliday's Party Girl

K ate loved the gambler-gunman Dr. John Holliday more than she loved any man. She loved the honkytonk-saloon-gambling-whoring life more than she loved any other way of life.

She was known as Kate Elder, although like many women in her trade, she went by many names, including Katherine, Katharine Michaels, and Katie Cummings. Wyatt Earp always referred to her as Katie Fisher. It was not unusual for a working girl to have a handful of sobriquets at her disposal. However, it was her professional nickname, Big Nose Kate, that set her apart from the other women in her line of work. Besides trying to hide one's true identity in a dodgy profession, a moniker was good for business because men tended to remember it. A girl had to stand out from the crowd, with names like Blonde Marie, Crazy Horse Lil, Molly B'Dam, Wicked Alice, Raunchy Rachael, and Squirrel Tooth Alice.

Kate had a slight German accent. She was born in Hungary in 1850 where her father was a successful physician to the aristocracy. He was asked to relocate to Mexico to take care of Maximilian I, so he uprooted the family. The family came to the New World around 1865. When the Mexican government crumbled, Kate's family barely made it out of Mexico alive and with little money. They moved to the United States, settling in Davenport, Iowa. Shortly thereafter, her mother died. A month later her father died. The Horony children were left in the custody of an uncle, and by 1870 they were wards of the state.

It appears that young Mary Katherine spent a few years at a Catholic school for girls. The structure didn't agree with her, though the education stuck and later served her well in a profession where most of her competitors were illiterate. Not liking her new foster family, Kate ran away from home. She may or may not have had a relationship with an older man. She may have married a medical man; we're not sure. At this time, Kate drops off the screen, and we get only hints of what might have become of her. Some suggest she married and had a child, but both child and father died in an outbreak of yellow fever. Some argue that she took up with a steamboat captain, making her way as best she could. At some point, she adopted the name of Fisher. She might have married or lived with a man of this name. At the least, it became one of her professional names, and she used it freely. At some point she became a prostitute. Being a quick study, she obviously learned the ways of the streets, saloons, and gambling houses and managed to make a comfortable living in a world that usually treated its victims indifferently. She also discovered that she loved gambling.

We do know that Kate Elder made her way to Dodge City, Kansas, in 1874, where she acquired the name of Big Nose Kate. When she first came to Dodge, she might have briefly worked for Nellie Earp, the common-law wife of Wyatt's brother James. Kate tried to recount some of her early history when she was older, but her recollections were convoluted. She drank a lot, and her memories must have been hampered by an alcoholic vapor. For example, she claimed that she and Doc went to Sweetwater, Texas, in 1875, but she was mistaken. Records indicate that she was a dance hall girl at Sherman's Dance Hall in Dodge at this time. She also said she married Doc in 1876, but that time doesn't square either. We have no record of her marrying Holliday at all, even though at one point she took his name and told everyone the two were wed.

Surely Doc and Kate had heard about each other before they shared drinks. Both had reputations in their own right. It's likely they crossed paths several times before they made sparks. Nightlife in frontier towns on the plains was not that big. They became officially acquainted in Fort Griffin, Texas, a wild town with few rules. It was a crossroads for any number of rough characters looking to blow off steam or to lay low from the law. The town was chock-full of brothels, gambling parlors, dance halls, and watering holes. It was a mecca for the likes of Kate and Holliday. Someone was always ready to try his hand at lady luck, drink cheap whiskey, or spend some time with the fairer sex. Kate liked Fort Griffin. Unlike many working ladies, she was an independent contractor. She didn't work for a pimp, nor did she often work for a madam. She could drink and gamble when she wanted to, she could earn good money dancing with a soldier or cowboy, or she could prostitute herself if she felt so inclined. She was likable and affable. She was not above standing a man to a drink and could tell dirty jokes. She knew when to laugh and when to listen. She had read the classics and could talk of Homer and the wine dark seas with a learned miner or sympathize with a cowboy's plight over the price of beef.

She liked the nightlife, but most of all she loved being independent. Other than a drunken bender every now and then, she was usually well behaved. Kate was well liked and knew enough important people that no one tried to corral her into a brothel or a pimp's string. Kate was reported to have an attractive physique, pretty hair, and a nice face. Her nose was a little large, but those who commented on her looks didn't think it detracted. One admirer said she had all the right curves. Men looked at her with longing—and she knew it.

During the later 1870s, she and Doc became friends. No doubt he had visited her professionally before they became close. It was also rumored that Wyatt Earp had visited her professionally. At some point, Kate and Doc fell for each other, and they became a working couple; he gambled, and she continued as a saloon girl, dancing for money, gambling, or visiting men in the back room. At the same time, Doc and Wyatt also became close friends, a friendship that would last until they left Tombstone. Holliday had helped Earp when things got testy with several difficult fugitives. Their relationship was cemented when Doc stepped in to help Earp

Kate Elder posed for this portrait around 1890 when she was close to forty. The effects of her hard life and harder drinking were starting to catch up with her.

COURTESY OF SHARLOT HALL MUSEUM LIBRARY AND ARCHIVES, PRESCOTT, ARIZONA.

during an altercation in a saloon. Wyatt was outnumbered. It looked grim for Earp until Holliday stepped in, offering his gun hand. Few men wanted to go up against Holliday because he didn't seem to care if he lived or died. Doc turned the tide, and Earp felt Doc had saved his life. Both men had a deep sense of romantic Southern honor. Earp felt in debt to the gambler. Soon after, Doc would feel this same sense of debt to Kate and Earp.

One evening in the fall, Holliday was playing cards with a man he discovered was cheating. Doc called him on it. The man drew his pistol and, reportedly, Doc sliced him with his knife. The man lay dead in a pool of blood on the floor. By western standards, cheating at cards was a shooting offense (or a slicing offense), since a card game was taken seriously. This had been a fair fight, so Holliday wasn't worried. The cheating was obvious to all those at the table. The problem was Holliday's reputation had followed him, and he had made enemies among those in high places. He was a known gunfighter. Even though the tinhorn drew on him first, the local law wasn't sympathetic. Officials thought this was an opportunity to take care of a problem, namely the gambler Doc Holliday. There wasn't a jail, so Holliday was disarmed and locked in his hotel room. A guard was posted at the door. A vigilante mob promoting law and order had been brewing, and some of the dead man's friends were calling for a Holliday hanging. Doc was starting to sweat.

Kate, having seen such mobs in action, was concerned about her lover's safety. The mood of the crowd was ugly. On the advice of Wyatt Earp, she went into action. Kate piled straw and pieces of wood near one of the buildings and poured a can of kerosene on the pile for extra measure. Probably with Earp's help, she collected a pair of saddle horses with traveling provisions. Kate always carried a gun and a knife, but she managed to procure a Colt .45 and proceeded toward Doc's room on the second floor of the hotel. On the way, she set a match to the straw and dry wood. Since the wood was dry, it burned like tinder. Before long, the call of fire rang out, and the town emptied out to fight the blaze. In a western town, fire was a dangerous threat. If the fire wasn't put out, it could ignite building after building, and a major portion of the town could burn to the ground. The townsmen and the mob left Doc in the hotel to go fight the fire. Kate slipped upstairs. The guard didn't argue with a cocked Colt pointed at his chest. Doc and Kate slipped into the night. There are several stories about how they escaped. One has them slipping out of town and hiding in the brush near a creek. In the morning, friends, perhaps Earp, brought them two horses and effected their escape. The other version, and the one that seems the most logical, is that two horses were tied near the hotel, and the lovebirds made their way into the night. Their destination was Dodge City, Kansas, where they hoped to make a new start.

Kate was a lively woman who's said to have liked her job. She certainly liked the independence it gave her. The hustle of the frontier nightlife, the tinny piano, the clink of glasses, the shuffle of cards, and the turn of the roulette wheel were sirens that drew her back to this way of life, again and again. For a while she was known as Mrs. John Holliday and enjoyed playing the respectable woman. After the near-death experience from the card game, the unlikely pair decided to go straight and live a conventional life. Holliday would do his dentistry, and Kate would be the doting housewife, a respectable woman in the community. She would see other women, drink tea, plant flowers, and prepare meals for Doc after he'd had a hard day of fixing teeth. Ironically, Kate was well educated and could act the part of civility, but she had a destructive streak. She could talk about the Lake poets, French history, or play the piano with her neighbors. However, old ways die hard, and she and Doc both were heavy drinkers, if not binge drinkers. It wouldn't do for the respectable dentist and his lady to be seen knocking back whiskey neat, putting a few dollars on the roulette wheel, or playing poker. Furthermore, no one had confidence in a dentist who closed down the bars and gambling houses—and smelled of whiskey as he worked his practice the next morning. After all, good women didn't go near drinking and gambling joints on the wrong side of the tracks. Eventually, Kate had had it with respectability and felt a bender coming on. She wanted to go back to where she felt comfortable. The polite, shallow society talk and weak English tea were too much. Starting to drink, she drank some more, gambled, and told vulgar jokes. Kate had a kind heart and a caring personality, but she could be an ugly drunk. After too much alcohol, she would say things she would regret. She'd spout personal stuff that she was sorry for saying after she sobered up—things that would embarrass Doc about his personal life.

After a drunken binge in Dodge City, when she could no longer stand to be respectable, Kate knew that she had committed social suicide; any chance she and Doc had of joining respectable society was shot. Doc had done his best to turn Kate into a respectable woman, but she was a party girl and a whore at heart. Their good name and Doc's practice had been trampled by Kate's drinking. Doc and Kate always managed to fight in public instead of behind closed doors. There was a huge, public blowup, one of many. The town knew Doc and Kate's business as they shouted and screamed. One of the fighting lovebirds would leave town for a while, but sooner or later they would kiss and make up.

It didn't seem to bother Holliday that Kate sold her body and was with other men. Nor was Kate offended by Doc's excessive drinking, marathon poker playing, or his almost obsessive relationship with Wyatt Earp. In Dodge, Doc was slowly declining, a victim of tuberculosis. Holliday had come out West where the air was dry. Besides his drinking, Doc discovered that few patients wanted a consumptive dentist who was coughing while he was working on them. Reportedly a good dentist, he traded his drill in for a deck of cards, a six-gun, and a Bowie knife. He had spells when he felt well, but he also had times when the consumption was very bad. It sent him into severe coughing fits that lasted for days. His friends noticed that his voice had become quieter and raspier. Sores had developed on the back of his throat, making it hard for him to talk above a whisper. The coughing spells were more frequent as he spit up pus and green mucus. In spite of their tumultuous relationship, when Holliday was suffering one of his sick spells, Kate was at her best. She stayed by his side and ministered to him. He appreciated her help because he was often so weak that he could not get out of bed. He needed her, and she needed him to need her.

After a particularly bad time, the pair decided to leave Dodge and head for Montezuma Hot Springs near Las Vegas, New Mexico. The sulfur waters were supposed to help those suffering from consumption. Accounts differ on when they left Dodge. Doc says they left as the snow was starting to fall, likely around the first of December. Their move may not have been precipitated simply by his health concerns. In order to get better control on gambling and prostitution, Dodge City officials had made Dodge a no-gambling, no-prostitution town—which adversely affected both of their

ARIZONA STATE BOARD OF HEALTH
BUREAU OF VITAL STATISTICS

STANDARD CERTIFICATE OF DEATH
DEPARTMENT OF COMMERCE
BUREAU OF THE CENSUS

State File No. 421
Registrar's No. 220.A

1. Place of Death: (a) County Yavapai (b) City or Town Prescott (c) Location Pioneer Home
(If outside city limits also write RURAL) (St. & No. (or) Name of Institution)

(d) Length of Stay: In Hospital or Institution 9 years In Community 9 years ; In Arizona 64 years
(Specify whether years, months or days)

2. Usual Residence of Deceased: (a) State Prescott ; (b) County Yavapai ; (c) City or Town Arizona
(d) Street No. Pioneer Home (If outside city limits also write RURAL)
(b) If foreign born (c) Social Security No. O (If NONE write the word)

3. (a) FULL NAME Mrs. Mary K. Cummings (b) If veteran name war.

4. Sex Female 5. Color or Race White 6. (a) Single, married, widowed Widow

MEDICAL CERTIFICATION

8. (b) Name of husband No record (c) Age of husband or wife, if alive yrs.

20. DATE OF DEATH (Month, day and year) Nov. 2, 1940
TIME (Hour and minute) 8:35 pm

7. Birthdate of deceased Nov. 7, 1850.
(Month) (Day) (Year)

8. AGE: Years 89 Months 11 Days 25 If less than one day hrs. min.

21. I hereby certify that I attended the deceased from Jan 3, 1938 to Nov 2, 1940; that I last saw her alive on Nov. 1, 1940; and that death occurred on the date and hour stated above.

9. Birthplace Davenport, Iowa.
(City, town or county) (State or Country)

Immediate cause of death. Acute myocardial insufficiency 1 day

DURATION

10. Usual Occupation At Home

Due to Coronary artery disease 3 months.

11. Industry or Business

12. Name Marchal H. Michael
13. Birthplace Unknown
(City, town or county) (State or Country)

Other conditions Advanced arteriosclerosis (Include pregnancy within 3 months of death) unknown

Major findings Of operations

PHYSICIAN

14. Maiden Name Catherine Baldwin
15. Birthplace Unknown
(City, town or county) (State or Country)

Of autopsy

Underline the cause to which death should be charged statistically.

16. (a) Informant's own signature Supt. Pioneer Home
(b) Address Prescott, Arizona.

22. If death was due to external causes, fill in the following:
(a) Accident, suicide or homicide (specify)
(b) Date of occurrence

17. (a) Burial, Cremation or Removal Burial
(b) Place Prescott, Ariz. Date Nov. 6, 1940

(c) Where did injury occur? (City or Town) (County) (State)
(d) Did injury occur in or about home, on farm, in industrial place, in public place?

18. (a) Embalmer's Signature Lester Ruffner
(b) Funeral Director Lester Ruffner
(c) Address Prescott, Arizona

(Specify type of place)
While at work? (c) Means of injury

19. (a) 11.3.40
(Date received local Registrar)
(b) Jno. F. McNally
(Registrar's Signature)

23. Signature N. J. [illegible] M. D.
Address Prescott, Arizona. Date signed Nov. 5, 40

5M 100% Aug 6/11/40

Big Nose Kate's official death certificate gives her name as Mrs. Mary K. Cummings and the cause of death as "acute myocardial insufficiency."
COURTESY ARIZONA DEPARTMENT OF HEALTH SERVICES.

professions. This new ordinance was not done out of a sense of morality, but out of civic pragmatism. The city fathers outlawed vice. Then they legalized it again but with stiff new taxes and regulations. This way the local government could collect steep taxes and have control over the brothels and gambling dens.

Holliday knew enough medicine to know what fate had in store—he'd been dealt a slow death sentence. Kate knew it, too. During his worst spells, she was with him. When he was feeling better, they fought. In his personal life, he was brash—what did he have to lose? A bullet in the chest would be easier than the slow strangling death that awaited him.

Back in Tombstone, after a long public argument during a 90-proof tirade, Kate indicated that Holliday might have been involved in a recent stage robbery. Already in a drunken state, she'd been fed drink after drink and coached by the sheriff to incriminate Doc. Sheriff Behan was the Earp brothers' and Doc Holliday's political enemy. He used Kate's inebriated babble to implicate Holliday for robbery and murder. He was trying to break the Earps' hold on Tombstone. While Doc was in jail, Kate sobered up, felt awful for what she had done, and recanted her testimony. The Earps then proved that Holliday was with a reputable witness during the robbery, and he was released from jail; however, he was angry with Kate. As a result, their relationship cooled off and was never the same. Holliday was taking long turns for the worse as his illness beat him up. They had forgiven each other many times, but this time Doc felt that Kate had betrayed him and was more trouble than she was worth. Rumor has it that he put her on a stage, gave her $1,000 so she could start over, turned his back, and walked away.

Reportedly, Kate made occasional visits to Tombstone and other towns to gamble and replenish her funds by practicing the oldest profession. Doc headed to Glenwood Springs, Colorado, to seek help at a sanatorium. It's not likely that Kate visited him while he was being treated. Kate moved around the West. Eventually, she married a man named Cummings, but the relationship didn't last. She ran a bakery and was known as Mrs. Mary K. Cummings. Around 1900, she moved to Cochise, Arizona, and worked at the Cochise Hotel until 1915. Later she kept house for John Howard until 1930. When Howard died, the Arizona governor, who was a personal friend, helped her gain admittance to the Arizona Pioneers Home. Just days before her ninetieth birthday, Kate died on November 2, 1940, from heart disease. ⇥

Big Minnie at the Bird Cage: The Big Girl in Pink Tights

In 1886, Joe Bignon and his wife, Maulda Branscomb, bought the Bird Cage Theater in Tombstone, Arizona. Maulda, known professionally as Big Minnie, was always part of the entertainment—whether she was on stage or not. Minnie was a part-time actress, a theatrical personality, a prostitute, a dancer, and a barmaid. Big Minnie got her name honestly. She weighed more than most prize fighters, topping the scales at 230 pounds, standing a solid six feet tall. And she was just as tough. Joe Bignon billed his wife as 230 pounds of loveliness in pink tights. It was not all fat, either. She packed muscles. Legend suggests that one night a drunk was out of line. He fired a shot that, fortunately, went innocuously into the ceiling. Someone suggested they call for the local law, but Minnie didn't want to bother. She wrapped a large arm around the man and lifted him over her shoulder, then flung him out the door. From that day forth, the Bignons saved money on a bouncer, and Minnie added it to her job description.

She kept a careful eye on the business' books and on her husband, who quickly learned his wife was nearly always right. Minnie also kept an eye on her customers and wanted them to spend money and have a good time. She was always ready if a customer wanted a beefy woman. The couple ran the Cage until the mines in Tombstone played out in 1890. Fortunately, a gold strike occurred in nearby Pearce. Ready to milk the next boom with a proven format, the enterprising couple opened up a new place called Joe Bignon's Palace. Many of their old friends and clients moved, too. Both Joe and Minnie played out their hands in Pearce and were buried in the local cemetery.

CHAPTER SIXTEEN

JOSEPHINE "SADIE" SARAH MARCUS

"Mrs." Wyatt Earp

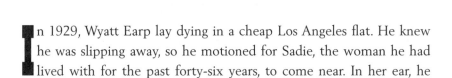

In 1929, Wyatt Earp lay dying in a cheap Los Angeles flat. He knew he was slipping away, so he motioned for Sadie, the woman he had lived with for the past forty-six years, to come near. In her ear, he whispered, "Suppose. Suppose."

He drew a rattled breath and was gone.

The legendary lawman, the big man who carried a badge from Dodge City to Tombstone, one of the most famous gunfighters in the West, passed, and so did a piece of the Old West. After a thousand saloon brawls, after facing desperate men with loaded guns, after fighting Comanche and blizzards, after the O.K. Corral, he hadn't received a scratch and had cheated death. Now death had tapped him on the shoulder, and he obeyed. He had been a lawman, a bounty hunter, a saloon owner, a brothel bouncer, a pimp, a gambler, and a prospector.

Forty some years earlier, Josephine, who was known as Sadie her entire adult life, had come to Tombstone, Arizona, with another man while Wyatt had commitments of his own. It was a long time ago, and it was never a subject they talked about publicly. The origin of their relationship was kept private. Most discussion on the subject is laced with a fair amount of speculation or is second hand.

Wyatt was a conflicted man. He was never satisfied and never quit chasing success. He had worked for the big money interests in both Dodge City and Tombstone and wanted to carve out a large piece of the American dream for himself. However, the next big strike or successful business venture always seemed to elude him. After Tombstone, he and Sadie went from boomtown to boomtown, looking for another El Dorado. Meanwhile, Wyatt gambled, and the couple made a living, but they never made it big. From Tombstone forward, the story of Wyatt and Sadie was the story of two strong-willed people who remained soul mates through the years, but it must not have been easy. Their lives were so intertwined that you can't talk about one without the other. Sadie was the love of his life, and he was the love of hers. Terry Earp, a great-nephew, said that "Wyatt and Josephine had their ups and downs like any other relationship between two people, but they were, however, devoted to one another, and their love survived their temperaments."

They met in Tombstone while Sadie was married, or more likely engaged to, and living with another man. Wyatt was living with his common-law wife, Mattie. We're not sure when the sparks started to fly between Wyatt and Sadie, but it was probably before the famous thirty-second gunfight at the O.K. Corral that occurred on October 26, 1881. That summer, on June 17, 1881, in his official capacity as a peace officer, Wyatt Earp issued a Tombstone City License to a certain Sadie Jo. On the business part of the license, Deputy Marshal Wyatt Earp had written "House of Ill Fortune" on Sixth and Allen SW. He charged her $7.50 for the right to do business in Tombstone. Sadie considered herself a dancer and an actress, but she found that she had to support herself between acting jobs. She worked under the professional names of Shady Sadie and Shady Jo.

Bat Masterson noticed Sadie when he was in Tombstone. He said she was the "Belle of the honkytonks, the prettiest dame in three hundred or so of her kind." Wyatt, who had always played fast and loose with the

The Bird Cage Theater: The Wickedest Place on Earth

In 1881, the folks around Tombstone needed a touch of culture, something to do between bouts of drinking and gambling. Enter the Bird Cage Theater. Yes, the Cage provided more drinking, gambling, and girls . . . but it also provided a cultural experience heretofore ignored. Never mind the 120-odd bullet holes in the ceiling and walls. There was something for everyone. There were fourteen cribs or "bird cages," little cubbies with a curtain and bed for those tempted by the naughty girls who were always ready to visit the nest. In the basement was one of the most famous poker

This 1937 image shows the Bird Cage Theater still in decent repair, though long past its prime years as the "Wickedest Night Spot between Basin Street and the Barbary Coast."
COURTESY LIBRARY OF CONGRESS, IMAGE 008722.

ladies, certainly noticed her, especially after he wrote her a business license. While he had lived with different women, he spent a good deal of his time in whorehouses, often as a bouncer or a pimp and playing cards on the side, since gambling was his second love. His brother James had married Nellie "Bessie" Bartlett Ketchum, a known prostitute and a madam with her own string of girls. At one time, Wyatt had surely been a regular customer. While on the plains, Wyatt had taken up with a prostitute named Mattie Blaylock. Some, including Mattie, said that she and Earp were married, but we can find no record of such a union. Likely Mattie was his common-law wife. As was the practice in that day for such a relationship, she took his name. Earp and Mattie lived together, but their games in the American West. It went for nearly eight straight years, twenty-four hours a day, seven days a week. The players changed, the money changed, but the game—poker—remained the same. It was said that $10,000,000 was wagered over the life of this giant game of chance (and don't forget 10 percent of the gross for the house).

The Cage was open 365 days a year, twenty-four hours a day. Like the poker game, the vice and the entertainment went on around the clock so all the shifts at the silver mines could join in. The *New York Times* said the Bird Cage was the "Wickedest Night Spot between Basin Street and the Barbary Coast."

When it came to classic entertainment, it was hard to beat the Human Fly, a daring woman who walked upside down across the ceiling of the theater. She brought the house down, until one evening she missed securing herself to one of the holes she had drilled in the ceiling, and she brought herself down, down to her death. And no one could forget the drunk who watched a cheesy melodrama and got too caught up in the theatrical moment. He was so worried about the dog chasing the protagonist, the inebriated patron pulled out his six-shooter and plugged the dog to help save the day. He didn't realize it was a highly trained dog—the man was too far over the limit to separate the finer points of the willing suspension of disbelief. Embarrassed, he sobered up in jail and paid for the damages. Then there was the woman who could catch coins thrown at her with her teeth. She lifted up her skirt and put the money in the top of her stockings. The house roared.

association didn't keep Earp from wandering, nor was the relationship particularly blissful. When they arrived in Tombstone, before they had a regular place to stay, they slept in a wagon. Wyatt gambled and performed his legal duties, including issuing licenses to working girls. Trying to earn extra money to supplement his marshal pay, Wyatt occasionally dabbled in real estate, among other ventures. He probably owned or rented a prime piece of business real estate to the well-known lady of the night, Dutch Annie. She built her famous house of ill repute on the lot. If he didn't sell her the land, he might have been one of her silent partners. The red light district was his second home.

For some time, while Wyatt was living with Mattie, he was having a serious relationship with the exciting Sadie, who was ten years his junior. Mattie knew about the relationship and was worried that this was more than a fling. She saw Wyatt drifting away from her by degrees. To get even, she displayed violent bursts of temper and started to drink heavily. She also used laudanum. As her emotional stability slipped, she begged Wyatt, sometimes publicly, to come back to her. Earp found her a burden and started living with his new love. Mattie dove further into the bottle.

Sadie was born in 1861 in Brooklyn, New York. Her parents were German-Jewish immigrants. Around 1870 or 1871, the family moved to San Francisco. Her father became a prosperous baker. He gave Sadie and her sister Hattie a wonderful education. This included acting and dancing classes. Bitten by the theatre bug, young Sadie would sneak out of the house and watch plays and theatrical performances in the city.

In her loosely constructed and whimsical biography, *I Married Wyatt Earp*, she suggests that she ran away from home when she was fourteen years old. Always a bit wild and high spirited, she was bored and wanted to see the world. She made her way to Prescott, Arizona, survived an Apache attack, and met the famous Indian scout Al Sieber, who took an instant liking to her. He, too, was of German ancestry. She learned that the lone and dreary world was more difficult than she'd imagined and was nothing like the Frisco stage. In her younger teenage years, there is a record that a "Sadie Mansfield" was charged for petty theft from a store. At a brothel located on Granite Street in Prescott, there is also an official mention of a young prostitute named Sadie. She was homesick and wanted to return to San Francisco. Al Sieber, the tough old army scout and Indian fighter, paid her way home.

By the time she was eighteen years old, she was bored and again left home to seek her fortune, perhaps a little older and a little wiser than before. The details of her career and life history remain a little vague. She toured with an acting troupe around Southern California doing *H.M.S. Pinafore*. Later the play was taken to cities and boomtowns in the Southwest. In her travels she met John Behan, who would later cross swords with Wyatt Earp. Apparently Behan was married at the time he met Sadie and was having difficulties with his wife. He and Sadie had a serious, or at least professional, relationship. John's wife, as Anne Butler records in *Daughters of Sin, Sisters of Misery*, was offended that her husband "openly and notoriously visited houses of ill-fame and a prostitute at said town of Prescott." She specifically named "Sada Mansfield as the favorite of Johnny's."

Victoria Behan filed for divorce. Johnny, with the young Sadie tucked up under his arm, headed for the exciting new town called Tombstone and a new horizon. Some have written that the couple was engaged, which is not verified. What is clear is that Sadie was associated with Behan. For a time she probably lived with Johnny while she was getting established. She soon took a job in a brothel, waiting for an acting position to open up. Johnny was made sheriff around 1879. This was a lucrative job since he was allowed to keep some of the taxes he collected. He became wealthy from fees and bribes. Johnny's administration was rife with graft. Wyatt Earp had wanted Behan's job, so there was some animosity between the two men to begin with. The sheriff's office and the U.S. marshal and his deputies were on a collision course. In 1881, Behan and Earp crossed paths. They took an instant dislike to one another. Perhaps at the center of this contention was one Josephine "Sadie" Marcus. It seemed that Johnny's girl, or former girl, had fallen for Wyatt Earp. At the same time, Wyatt made public his concerns about the sheriff's misappropriation of funds. The two lawmen had several verbal altercations over Sadie.

Wyatt had fallen for the actress-working girl, and he wanted her. In the meantime, Mattie was suffering from depression and was using heavier and heavier doses of laudanum to self-medicate, which added to her already unstable personality. As a result, Mattie had violent fits of public temper. On other occasions, she had a hard time standing without falling. She became a public spectacle and the butt of many jokes. Wyatt hated sentimentality and how she humiliated him in public. He wished to keep their dissolving love life private. Her loud public shouting matches in saloons and gambling houses were embarrassing to a man who was trying to work his way up the ladder. Her efforts to make the problems public only drove a deeper wedge into the relationship. Mattie threatened suicide. Such actions alienated Wyatt even further. When he started to live with Sadie, the infuriated Mattie played the abused wife.

Before long, Mattie fell under the dark spell of opium and eventually moved to California, hoping Wyatt would follow her. Of course, he never did. During the shootout at the O.K. Corral, maybe the most overhyped gunfight in history, Wyatt's brother Morgan was shot in the shoulder. His other brother Virgil took a bullet in the leg. Doc Holliday was grazed on the hip. All three men recovered from their wounds. Wyatt walked away without a scratch. Three cowboys, however, weren't so lucky. Tom McLaury, Frank McLaury, and Billy Clanton lay dead at the corral. Two months later, Virgil Earp was ambushed and shot in the shoulder, permanently losing the use of his left arm. In March 1882, Morgan Earp was gunned down while he was shooting billiards. He was shot in the right side, and his spine was shattered. As a lawman, Wyatt Earp went out to even the score in a sort of Old Testament vendetta. He used his badge as a tool to seek revenge. He hunted down the murderers, brutally riding over anyone who got in his way. He took the law into his own hands and settled the debt. He felt he had done the right thing, but his methods turned the public against him, and he was looked upon as a murderer.

Earp's reputation plummeted, and warrants were sworn against him. He couldn't understand how quickly public opinion turned. He and Sadie spent the rest of their lives trying to find public vindication for Tombstone. After leaving Tombstone, the town changed as the mine started to play out, and the boomtown lost its edge. Nothing was the same. Big Nose Kate Elder was splitting with Doc Holliday, and there was little money to be made. Wyatt's brothers had been shot up, and his relationship with Doc Holliday was cooling. In 1888, the *Arizona Enterprise* reported that Mattie Blaylock, "a frail denizen of Pinal [Arizona]" died from an overdose of laudanum.

Sadie and Wyatt wandered the West, following the big money in boomtowns, marshaling, bartending, and, always, gambling. On cards, horses, dice—any game of chance.

As we've learned, both Wyatt and Sadie were mysterious, if not guarded, about their Tombstone years. Wyatt felt he'd been victimized by the press in the last days of Tombstone and that his reputation had been tarnished by slanted reporting. He also felt that those he had supported had turned against him when they should have been defending him. He and Sadie felt he was not a murderous killer cloaked by his badge, but a keeper of law and order. He hoped that at some point he might be vindicated.

Wyatt wanted to tell the true story of his life (and have it understood), but at the same time he wanted to protect Sadie's reputation by leaving out any mention of her prostitution. He felt that he, and not Sadie, was the issue in this drama. He sheltered her. He did not want the press to do to Sadie what it had done to him. It was as if the couple drew a cloak over parts of her life so no one would see the truth. In 1928, Wyatt urged Billy Breckinridge, former deputy sheriff of Cochise County, to keep Wyatt's relationship with Sadie out of Breckinridge's forthcoming book, *Helldorado: Bringing Law to the Mesquite.* After Wyatt's death in 1929, Sadie continued Wyatt's badgering by threatening a legal battle with Breckinridge if he wrote about her. That same year, Sadie tried to stop the publication of Stuart Lake's *Wyatt Earp: Frontier Marshal.*

Feeling a financial pinch after Wyatt's death, Sadie decided to write her memoirs about her life with Earp, *I Married Wyatt Earp.* Several publishers were interested in her manuscript, but in the final analysis she was too difficult to work with, and no publisher wanted to take on the project. Later on she tried again to market her book. Another publisher thought her story had merit, but he backed out because Sadie, as she had been with previous publishers, was too close-lipped about important aspects of her life in Tombstone. Again, she wasn't willing to make additions or add necessary changes to her text. In addition, some of the text, according to her editor, went from historical flaws to outright lies—which is an accurate assessment. As Wyatt had tried to protect her past, she felt an obligation to defend, if not glorify, the Earp legend. She wanted Wyatt portrayed as a man who stood for law and order, the man who brought order to frontier towns in the Wild West—not as a man who used his badge to promote his own self-interests. She wanted the text to portray her as the loving wife, whitewashing her prostitute past. Sadie wanted to be known as the loving woman behind the hero with the badge.

Her reluctance to capitulate was unfortunate. Western movies, Western biographies, and Western novels were big business. The Earp legend had nearly gone full circle, and Wyatt, thanks to recent books and Hollywood, was regarded as a law and order man. Disillusioned about her failure to publish her manuscript, however, she ordered all copies to be burned. One of Wyatt's cousins, Mabel Earp Cason, not wanting to see the text destroyed, kept a copy; Cason later sold the copy to Glen Boyer, who turned it into a bestseller. It was an interesting book, but the scholarship was false, flawed, or carelessly presented. Later, Boyer admitted that he made up large sections of the text to fill in the blanks (some of these were blanks Sadie had refused to comment on).

Later, when Frank Walters was writing his book, *The Earp Brothers*, Sadie again tried to strong-arm the author by threatening his family with legal action. She felt she was fighting for Wyatt's reputation, keeping some of the facts of their early life together from coming out. In 1939, *Wyatt Earp: Frontier Marshal* was made into a movie.

Sadie wisely accepted the offer to consult on the script and provide background material. Desperately in need of money, she capitulated. She must have thought, who better to set the record straight? She was the woman who had lived it. Sadie received royalties from the movie, but the money didn't last long. What she didn't lose in games of chance, she drank up. Wyatt didn't live to see the vindication of his reputation, but during the last part of Sadie's life and after her death, Earp finally, if not falsely, became the legendary symbol of law and order he had struggled to be perceived as. Instead of a disillusioned, heavy-handed lawman with fingers in prostitution and gambling, a man who sold favored special interests, Wyatt became the lawman who brought order to the chaos of the lawless West.

Broken but proud, Sadie died in her eighties in Los Angeles. She was buried next to Wyatt in Colma, California, in her family plot. She had seen the Wild West. She had rubbed shoulders with the famous and infamous characters in our history. She'd been an actress, a prostitute, a dance hall girl, and the companion of one of the most famous men of the nineteenth century. ⊶

CHAPTER SEVENTEEN

DOLLY ARTHUR

A Girl from Idaho and the Queen Madam of Ketchikan

In an Alaskan mist as the late afternoon fog rolls into Ketchikan, it's easy to picture the Creek Street boardwalk packed with miners, loggers, and fishermen. These were hardworking men, blowing off steam in the red light district. Creek Street was known as "the Barbary Coast of the North," and, as Ketchikan writer Dave Kiffer says, "the place where men and fish go upstream to spawn." In a speech to Congress, one concerned Alaska Territory delegate, Dan Sutherland of Juneau, went so far as to say that Ketchikan was the most morally corrupt town in America. Indeed, seemingly every vice was available: gambling, alcohol, narcotics, and loose women. Perhaps thirty houses of prostitution nestled on a boardwalk that stretched across Ketchikan Creek. Technically, it was illegal for bawdy girls to ply their trade on the land in city limits, so the boardwalk was a handy way to sidestep the technicalities of the law. In some respects, Creek Street today still looks like it did at the turn of the century. Of course, the boards are more weathered, and some of the

At the time of Dolly's arrival, Ketchikan numbered about 2,000 souls strung along the steep shoreline of Tongass Narrows.
PHOTOGRAPH BY A. H. BROOKS, COURTESY U.S. GEOLOGICAL SURVEY.

buildings are gone. The working girls are gone, too, but the walk is still slippery in the misty sea air.

Raw sewage, bottles, and other debris are no longer dumped in the creek to be washed out at high tide—a tide that has also washed more than one dead body out to sea under mysterious circumstances. Today, tourists from cruise boats and other visitors pack the boardwalks in the summer. At the end of the walk, you can see where Annie Watkins and her girls entertained. It was a whorehouse; it's now a restaurant. Black Mary owned the Star, and Dolly Arthur set up her sole proprietorship at #24. For the record, she claimed that she worked until the state of Alaska made her profession illegal in 1953. Off the record, she suggested she plied her trade much longer.

Dolly Arthur's real name was Thelma Dolly Copeland. She was born in the Idaho mining district in 1888. Young Thelma had a tragic child-hood. As a girl she was the victim of savage and repeated sexual abuse. As a woman she suggested that she was never worried about becoming

It was illegal in Ketchikan to have a house of prostitution in city limits, so enterprising women set up their businesses on the boardwalk of Creek Street, which was outside city limits. COURTESY OF KETCHIKAN MUSEUMS: TONGASS HISTORICAL COLLECTION, SIXTEN JOHANSON IMAGE, THS 70.7.26.11.

pregnant because the brutal sexual abuse had made conception impossible. To escape her situation, she left home when she was thirteen. She took odd jobs in Montana and around the West. She worked as a waitress. A beautiful young woman, Dolly was pleasant and good with customers. She heard a number of marriage proposals and had plenty of interested men chasing her skirts, but she was not interested. Before she was twenty, she found herself in British Columbia. She commented, "By the time I was 18 or 19 I realized that I could make more money from the attention of men than by waiting on tables."

She later said, "I just like men and they like me." At some point in her late teens, she gave up her apron, taking food orders, and dishrags, vowing to never again wait tables for a living. She stayed in the service industry, but the menu was different. It would be interesting to know how the transition occurred. But we know that she said prostitution was a financial decision. She was not forced into prostitution like so many; she chose it. She was poor as a waitress, but she wasn't destitute. Furthermore, a number of men were interested in her hand, and she could easily have been a wife. She had options. She chose this profession because the money was good, even if the working conditions left a lot to be desired. We don't know much more about her early life. She gave a number of interviews when she was older, but these parts were left unexplained. We know she went to Vancouver in her twenties and had a serious relationship that turned out badly and left her heartbroken.

Dolly was shapely and on the large side. She also had a temper and a foul mouth. At the same time, she had a sentimental streak and enjoyed helping the down and out. She grubstaked many a man and was considered a good friend by most of her callers. After her heartbreak, she wanted adventure and desperately needed a change. The north had plenty of men, so in 1919 she sailed for Ketchikan, Alaska, ready for a new life. Little did she know that the Last Frontier would become her home. Alaska agreed with her.

Dolly went to work for Black Mary at the Star. She stayed at the Star for a year while she saved money. She had previously worked for Mary, and the two were good friends. Mary had bought the Star in 1917 for $4,000 and was probably instrumental in relocating Dolly to Ketchikan. Dolly watched Mary work and learned a lot about the business side of their profession. Mary was an astute businesswoman, and the Star turned a fine profit. Dolly also saw Mary invest her money—something most prostitutes rarely did. Most spent their earnings on clothes, but Mary made her own clothes and lived modestly. Unlike most madams, Mary had the respect of her girls. Later, when Black Mary died, Dolly was deeply saddened at the loss of her close friend. Throughout her life, when Mary's name was mentioned, Dolly would tear up.

There were no hard feelings when Dolly decided to go into business for herself. Dolly had Mary's blessings. After the sexual cruelty of her youth, she needed to be in control, likely due to trust issues. Dolly always valued independence. Furthermore, as a businesswoman, Dolly was also aware of the laws of the Alaska Territory and felt safe as a solo act. In those days, a house of prostitution was defined as having three or more women under one roof. Strictly speaking, a house with just one or two women was a "residence" and not subject to the same legal sanctions as brothels. For the rest of her career she worked alone. She registered her legal business with the local police and worked her trade.

Ketchikan's red light district was on Creek Street, built over the water of Ketchikan Creek near where it empties into Tongass Narrows. When high tide came in, litter and sewage were carried out to sea. COURTESY COURTESY OF KETCHIKAN MUSEUMS: TONGASS HISTORICAL COLLECTION, THS 74.7.4.19.

Dolly bought #24 Creek Street for $800. It was a small house but perfect for her needs. The downstairs had a dining room, a parlor, and a secret hiding place for her liquor during Prohibition. The upstairs had two bedrooms and a bathroom. At some point, she had a carpenter join the two bedrooms into a larger single. She was a careful businesswoman. Dolly kept meticulous records, which was an added protection against harassment. She had every man who visited her sign her registry, which she guarded carefully. When she opened for business, she charged $3 for a visit. The average working girl made a little over a dollar a day at that time. Unlike some of the girls, she kept a low profile and was not flamboyant.

In the 1920s, business was especially good for the girls on the creek. Brothels and prostitutes charged premium prices for alcohol, so Prohibition brought them extra prosperity. Most women made more from the drinks

The Evolution of a Boomtown: From Bawdy to Proper

Bawdy women, tawdry gambling joints, and plentiful drinking establishments were welcomed in boomtowns, whether the boom was mining, the railroad, cattle, or logging. Boomtowns shared a few things in common: a lot of men, gambling, drinking, and very few women. Feminine companionship, even if the meter was running, was a desired commodity. Few thought of social conventions or the proper etiquette for laying out an afternoon tea. These men were pioneering vanguards. They embraced the rugged frontier, clinging to the dream of wealth or the hope of a new life. They faced unthinkable hardships and dangers. They lived in tents or flimsy housing with none of the comforts of home. They worked hard and they played hard when they got to town—a town that, at least at its inception, was little more than canvas tarps, planks across barrels for a bar, rough-hewn tables, and cots for beds. Many spent their month's earnings on a single wild night.

As a town prospered, women and churches arrived and started the painful process of civilization. The vices that had been embraced wholeheartedly became a source of embarrassment. Town fathers who publicly bent to the voice of propriety were reluctant to lose the municipal revenue from licenses and taxes on vice. Nor did they want to lose the business of those who frequented the shady side of town after dark but also frequented stores and proper businesses during the day. Many western states (Wyoming, for instance) and cities funded local schools from taxes on prostitution. Other vice taxes, licenses, and fees underwrote many civic projects.

they peddled than from services rendered. Alaska officials didn't much care for the national liquor law, but there was a token resistance, enough to keep the prices inflated. Bootlegged liquor was brought in at night during high tide. Large boats kept out of sight during the day and slipped in close at night. Row boats brought the merchandise up the creek to the boardwalk. Many of the bigger saloons and houses had trap doors beneath the floors to make unloading easier and quicker. During the Great Depression, the economic pace slowed nationally, but southeast Alaska was the salmon capital of the world, so fishermen and cannery workers were always working.

After the turn of the century, Ketchikan, Alaska, was growing. Women's groups and churches insisted that sin and vice be moved from town, that the docks and front street be cleaned up. It was no longer shacks and tents and bars and easy virtue. Under pressure, city fathers passed a petition that prostitutes be moved from city limits. The world's oldest profession, however, didn't have to go far. Virtue was its own reward, but the city fathers were also pragmatic businessmen. Miners, sailors, fishermen, and loggers needed supplies the local merchants were eager to sell. But such buyers would take their business to another port if there weren't diversions. To make local women and the church leaders happy, prostitutes were removed a very short distance to the other side of the creek into what was then called Indian Town.

Most towns followed a similar pattern. Prostitution and other vices couldn't be wiped out, but they could be isolated and controlled . . . and taxed. As a town grew respectable, the vices were often moved just outside city limits or to an isolated part of town. Terms such as the red light district, hell's half acre, the wrong side of the tracks, the line, among others, were used to identify the shady, dodgy parts of town. In many communities, women from the red light districts were not allowed in the respectable parts of town. Or, as in the early days of Ketchikan, bawdy women were allowed to shop only during certain hours on prescribed days. Proper women stayed home during these hours. If perchance a prostitute were to meet a respectable woman, she wasn't allowed to look at, greet, or talk to her. Such an offense might earn her a seat on the next outbound stage, ship, or train.

As Alaska moved from the frontier to the atomic age with the defeat of Japan and Germany, legalized prostitution began to be an embarrassment for territorial residents. Dolly, who had been in business at #24 for thirty years, must have noticed the change, too. Gone were the rip-roaring days of Alaska's youth. The wild recklessness of the first wave of pioneers was also gone. Proper wives, the clergy, and civic leaders were assuming an air of morality that left little room for legalized prostitution. These groups argued that prostitution, especially in Ketchikan, should not be sanctioned by the government—especially if Alaskans were trying to gain statehood.

Local women's groups took the lead. Their mantra was "Men often make a mess of things and leave it to the women to clean up." Prostitution in the last frontier started to draw national attention, which was the kind of notoriety the civic-minded did not want. In 1953, it became illegal. Dolly officially shut her door, but claimed that, unofficially, she remained open to favorite customers. In an interview, Dolly said she practiced her profession until she was seventy, but we can take that with a grain of salt. It's reasonable to believe that she practiced her trade for almost fifty years. It was not a secret what she did for a living. As she got older, she was more of a reminder of the frontier days than a scarlet woman. She was the symbol of the old, wicked Ketchikan, but those days were also looked back upon with nostalgia. Enough time had passed that she came to represent the romance of the boomtown. She was of the old stock, rugged and tough. She outlived her past and Creek Street.

In the late 1970s, she started to grow weak and finally had to leave her beloved home and go into a nursing facility. Finally, in 1975 she passed away at the age of eighty-seven . . . the last of her kind. ⇥

BIG DOROTHY
The Last of the Old-Time Madams

There's rumor that "Big Dorothy" Baker's ghost wanders her bawdy house seeking solace. Decades after the final raid on the old brothel at 19½ South Last Chance Gulch, folks with paranormal talents (of which I have none) have suggested that the 120-year-old building in Helena, Montana, might still host "spirited" activities. Simply put, maybe the old whorehouse is haunted by ghosts from Montana's past? Some believe the big madam herself roams the rooms she knew so well during mortality. This begs the next question: Is her spirit unable to find rest?

Most who believe in extra-world activity agree that her ghost is friendly; such folk have speculated that "Big Dorothy" simply wants Helena to know she has not fully passed to her reward. After all, she died before she had her day in court, before she could exonerate herself. Whatever the reason, strange activities are afoot in her old "rooms" and the surrounding structure on Last Chance Gulch, which nowadays hosts a fine restaurant called the Windbag Saloon. Those in tune with the paranormal world have reportedly heard soft music and laughter, as well as ladies' voices. Yet, when someone investigates, these rooms are strangely empty. Never mind that the sound system in the restaurant is known to inexplicably change channels when no one is near the receiver. Could "Big Dorothy" tire of classic rock or country music? Is this her way of making her presence known?

Even more puzzling, some visitors swear if you take a deep breath, you can sometimes smell the waft of old-time perfume (the kind Dorothy and her ladies wore to entertain gentlemen callers). And if you are brave enough to be in the building late at night when the crowds are gone and the place is quiet and lonely, be careful when you look up at the big mirror above the bar. Maybe you're not the only being in the room. In the sallow reflection of the old watering hole, you might see someone walking toward you in a friendly fashion. Naturally, without thinking, you'll turn around to greet your visitor . . . but when you do, no one is there. If a cold shiver doesn't run down your back, you have nerves as icy as the water in a mountain trout stream. Puzzled, you'll have to admit it *appears* no one is there, but you know you are not alone. Did you see a ghost?

But it doesn't end here. It seems Madam Dorothy, popular woman that she was in life, might still have visitors, favorite callers who, too, have not settled well into that good night. One evening, a pretty customer at the restaurant swore she saw an attractive, trail-dusty cowboy in a bandanna and a dust jacket saunter through the door toward "Dorothy's Rooms" while she was having dinner. He looked as if he was off a trail drive. Their eyes met, and he politely touched his hat as a token of respect. Then he was gone. The young lady pointed out the handsome cowhand to her husband, who was looking in the same direction. He insists he never saw the fellow. Some wonder if he was a spirit caller, a ghost rider, coming to visit the brothel after his drive?

Folks have to decide for themselves. Maybe a walk along Last Chance Gulch will be enough to convince you. Many paranormal explorers have lunch in the Windbag Saloon and spend the rest of the day wandering around the building before the evening crowd drifts in. My experience as a ghost buster was lackluster. The stereo didn't change channels and all I saw in the mirror was my aging face. I don't typically believe in ghosts, but I was prepared to be converted. Sadly, I never heard voices, smelled perfume, or saw a ghost. Maybe next time!

In life and in death, Madam "Big Dorothy" Baker was the last of her

Dorothy's Rooms occupied the second story of the Boston Block (building on left) on Last Chance Gulch in downtown Helena, Montana. This 1974 photograph shows the building during Urban Renewal, the winter following Dorothy's death.
COURTESY KENNON BAIRD.

breed, the last of the old-time madams. The West dies hard in mining and cattle country, especially in Helena, Montana. To the delight of the residents, most of the modern world had not yet caught up with Helena in the 1970s. In fact, in this historic city, the twentieth century was dragged unwillingly across the mountains and plains like a hog-tied steer. Spurs and Colt revolvers and dusters and whiskey neat were never out of place. "Big Dorothy" did business the way it had been done for over a century. She was a conspicuous part of the community, but she wasn't pushy. Her public manners were never vulgar or exaggerated. She helped and supported community causes and was generous and kind with her money. She felt connected to Helena. Her establishment was even listed in the phonebook as "Dorothy's Rooms." She would also advertise by visiting the local bars, buying a round of drinks for the house courtesy of "Big Dorothy."

Ironically, while she is arguably one of the most famous madams in Montana history, we know shockingly little about her personal life. She kept it private. What we do know are a few sketchy vignettes. She was born Dorothy Putnam, probably in Great Falls, Montana, but like most women in her trade, she adopted a professional handle: "Big Dorothy," a name that was easy for clients to remember. The name was apropos since she was a larger-framed woman, topping the scale at nearly 250 pounds. A name change also helped her avoid embarrassing her family. She dropped Putnam and called herself Dorothy Josephine Baker. The middle name was in honor of "Chicago Joe," Josephine Airey, a famous Montana brothel keeper from the previous century. We're not completely sure where the last name of Baker came from, but speculation suggests it might be in honor of a "Baker" Bread delivery truck.

We don't know which month she was born or the year, although it was likely in 1916. We also know that in her Great Falls High School yearbook she signed her name as "Dodie." We know she was close to her sister, Margaret, and her brother-in-law. As an aunt, Dorothy doted on her niece and nephew, even paying for their college educations. She remained close to her sister throughout her life. They visited frequently. The two had a traditional Catholic upbringing, and Margaret, before marrying, considered joining a convent. Obviously Margaret knew what her sister did for a living, but her profession didn't affect their relationship.

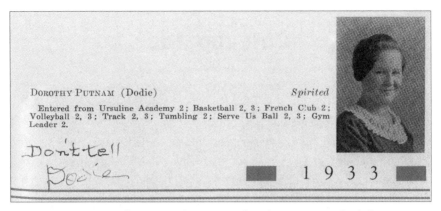

DOROTHY PUTNAM (Dodie)   *Spirited*

Entered from Ursuline Academy 2; Basketball 2, 3; French Club 2; Volleyball 2, 3; Track 2, 3; Tumbling 2; Serve Us Ball 2, 3; Gym Leader 2.

Don't tell

Dodie

■ ■ 1 9 3 3 ■

Dorothy Putnam was characterized as "Spirited" in her senior yearbook from Great Falls High School in 1933. Presaging her future career, Dorothy helped organize the school's "Serve Us Ball" dance. 1933 GREAT FALLS HIGH SCHOOL YEARBOOK, PAGE 53., Z371.8976, MONTANA HISTORICAL SOCIETY RESEARCH CENTER, ARCHIVES.

After the end of World War I, the moral purity movement swept across the country. Prohibition became the law of the land. The repercussions were also felt in the red light and vice districts. Although illegal, prostitution in many cities was openly practiced. Houses were occasionally raided, and ladies of the evening were carried off to jail with fanfare. Such actions kept the control of lucrative vice districts in the palms of the local municipalities via fines, licenses, and bribes. And just as important, such perfunctory raids—busts executed with a surgical morality—were good for media exposure, showing the conservative electorate that city officials were doing their best to "clean up" the community. With the new change of direction, prostitution and other vice industries were pushed underground. They would resurface again, of course, but the overt manner of doing business-as-usual was over.

The vice industry by necessity had to re-tool itself. As a rule, it would be relegated to specific districts, or masked, growing a newer, more innocuous politically correct handle. Creative euphemisms served as doublespeak, disguising the product or service from the community reformer or the average churchgoing citizen, but identifying the product or service for the willing consumer. Semantically it seems rather silly today. But out of sight and relabeled was out of mind. For example, during Prohibition liquor might be referred to as "tea" or "lemonade." In the prostitution business, a brothel

Chicago Joe

"**C**hicago Joe" took the American dream by the throat and lived the good life for several decades as a successful madam and businesswoman in Helena, Montana. She was born Mary Welsh in Ireland. When she was fourteen years old, her family immigrated to the United States, leaving their damp homeland, a land of little opportunity, behind. Mary worked at a number of jobs in New York before relocating to Chicago and becoming a prostitute. A likable young tart, she changed her name to Josephine Airey because she enjoyed how it sounded.

Her Irish charm and polite, straightforward ways set her apart in a business that was noted for crooked, underhanded dealing. Her philosophy was simple: There was more money in management, and you needed to

be fair with your clients. Young Josephine opened up a small brothel that proved successful. With her girls, she set the record straight on how they were going to do business. She was firm, but honest. She expected her painted ladies to treat their clients fairly.

After saving a sizable nest egg, she moved west to Montana.

Her destination was a boomtown named Helena. The town was pretty rough when she got there, but she saw possibilities in the rough-hewn houses and pitched tents. It was hot in the summer, cold in the winter, and whenever it rained, the streets were seas of mud. Most important, the mines provided a good wage for the workers, and there were men who needed female company.

Josephine wasn't adverse to risking her assets on business ventures. She proved to have good business sense. Indeed, at one time she was the largest property owner in Helena. In the 1870s, there was a fire on her street, and a number of businesses were wiped out. She bought the charred property and speculated in real estate. By the time she was thirty, the former Mary Welsh was a rich woman. At some point in her early Montana days, Josephine picked up the nickname she would have for the rest of her life, "Chicago Joe." "Joe" was surely clipped from Josephine, and it was understood she'd come from Chicago.

Chicago Joe's main brothel in Helena was The Grand, a stately, mansard-roofed brick building on the corner of Bridge (now State Street) and Joliet (near today's Cruse Street). The Grand was demolished in the 1970s.
COURTESY OF THE SEAN LOGAN COLLECTION.

would not be overtly advertised or referred to; instead it would be called something more innocent. By the time "Big Dorothy" was in the business, she became a master of doublespeak and euphemism. Prostitution got clever, so that advertising, even in the family telephone books, seemed legitimate. While in previous days it might be called Dorothy's Whore House, Bawdy House, or Hell's Half Acre, new terms like "Upstairs Rooms," "Furnished Rooms," or "Rooms" became the more acceptable language.

Dorothy probably entered into her profession in her late teens or early twenties. At one time she worked for a well-known madam named Pearl Maxwell. Later, she was employed by Madam Ida Levy at 19½ South Main Street (later Last Chance Gulch). The two became good friends. Ida, who was quite a local character, cut a popular figure in Helena nightlife. She also had a sense of humor. It was her habit to go to her favorite high-end clothing store and order expensive, custom ties for her best customers. It became a game with the employees at the clothing store to see which prominent citizens in Helena would show up in one of Ida's gifts. Dorothy learned the business aspects of prostitution from her mentor. When Ida retired in the early 1950s, "Big Dorothy," already a permanent fixture at the "rooms," took over the business and ran it successfully until 1973 when she was shut down by law enforcement. "Big Dorothy" had ridden out several police raids and a number of threats by zealous district attorneys before. By brothel standards, she remained relatively untouched by the local establishment. She had friends in high places who helped, but she also maintained a low profile while trying to do things that benefited the community. Dorothy finally tripped up when she ran afoul of federal regulations on Urban Renewal.

Downtown Helena had become rundown. Civic minded and eager to rekindle business (especially her own), she applied for and received a $500 Urban Renewal grant to fix up her building. She had friends who helped pencil-whip the grant through channels of red tape. After close consideration, and after the money was spent, the action drew criticism. Dorothy's detractors felt the federal grant should have been spent on legitimate retail business, not remodeling a whorehouse. Dorothy Baker's action created a political headache. The mayor, who drew fire, conveniently suggested he was out of town when the application was processed and knew nothing about it. Officials and decision makers were criticized and quick to defend or deflect blame. The local district attorney who had Madam Baker in his sights was ready to act. He sent an undercover policeman to visit her parlor. The cop paid one dollar for a drink—Dorothy didn't have a liquor license—and then he paid a girl to undress on her bed and perform lewd gestures. That was all the evidence the D.A. needed to proceed: She was selling liquor without a license, she was operating a house of prostitution, and she had violated federal law. On April 17, 1973, with a writ of injunction, she was raided. An admirer in local government had tipped her off, so most of her girls were not on the premises. When the police busted her rooms, Dorothy answered the door personally but was unprepared for what would happen next. This time the law was serious. The lawmen were under direct orders from the district attorney to close it down . . . this time for good. The windows and doors were boarded. Dorothy and one of her employees (who was hiding) were physically removed from the premises.

Whore she might be, whorehouse she might run; nevertheless, "Big Dorothy" Baker was still a popular woman in Helena with friends (and skeletons). The mayor had distanced himself, but other town officials were not so cagey. They openly opposed the raid, as did some of the citizens of Helena. Letters of support sent to the local papers were an indication of the local feelings about the raid. It was the buzz of the town. For many citizens, the rooms on Last Chance Gulch were an icon of Helena's past. The lovable old madam was a link, albeit a mysterious one, to the glorious rough-and-tumble days of the Wild West, an Old West that was about to pass. No one was more outspoken or critical than Helena City Commissioner Ed Lorunz, who knew Dorothy personally.

"She's always been a fine woman," he said. "She was always doing something for somebody. She'd lend you money. She'd tip the police off to drug pushers. I remember when a ladies service organization here called [her with a problem]. They said they had a crippled boy who they wanted to send to college and would she help. As I understood it, she wrote out a check right there."

Letters supporting Dorothy continued to flood the *Helena Independent Record*. However, before the madam could have her day in court, Big Dorothy fell ill. She had not been in good health and suffered with diabetes. No doubt the stress of her arrest and the fact that she didn't take good care of herself were contributing factors. She was taken to the hospital at Great Falls. She would never leave. Her situation worsened, and she passed on to her reward.

Dorothy's legacy lives on in Helena. Last Chance Gulch is still frequented by visitors. They hope Dorothy or a friendly apparition will make its presence known. If you visit the Gulch and listen very carefully in the wee hours of the night, maybe you will hear soft laughter or smell the hint of perfume—or imagine that you do. ⊷

BIBLIOGRAPHY

Abbott, Edith. *Women in Industry: A Study in American Economic History.* New York: D. Appleton and Co. 1918.

Aldridge, Dorothy. *Historic Colorado City: A Quick History, The Town with a Future.* Colorado Springs: Little London Press. 1996.

Armitage, Susan, and Elizabeth Jameson, editors. *The Women's West.* Norman: University of Oklahoma Press. 1987.

Billington, Ray Allen. *America's Frontier Heritage.* New York: Holt, Rinehart and Winston. 1966.

Brown, Larry K. *Petticoat Prisoners of Old Wyoming.* Glendo: High Plains Press. 2001.

Brown, Robert L. *Colorado Ghost Towns Past and Present.* Caldwell: Caxton Printers. 1981.

Bullough, Vern L. *The History of Prostitution.* New York: University Books. 1964.

Butler, Anne M. *Daughters of Joy, Sisters of Misery: Prostitutes in the American West 1865-90.* Chicago: University of Illinois Press. 1985.

Butler, Anne M., and Ona Siporin. *Uncommon Common Women: Ordinary Lives of the West.* Logan: Utah State University Press. 1996.

Clarke, Charles G. *The Men of the Lewis and Clark Expedition.* Glendale: Arthur H. Clark Co. 1970.

Clemens, Samuel L. (Mark Twain). *Roughing It.* Hartford: American Publishing Co. 1872. PDF ebook.

Dary, David. *Seeking Pleasure in the Old West.* Lawrence: University Press of Kansas. 1995.

Davis, Ronald L. *A History of Music in American Life: The Formative Years, 1620-1865.* Malabar: Robert Krieger Publishing Co. 1982.

Day, James et al. *Women of Texas.* Waco: Texan Press. 1972.

Dial, Scott. *Saloons of Denver.* Ft. Collins: The Old Army Press. 1973.

Finnegan, Frances. *Poverty and Prostitution: A Study of Victorian Prostitutes in York.* Cambridge: Cambridge University Press. 1979.

Flexner, Abraham. *Prostitution in Europe.* New York: The Century Co. 1920.

Goldman, Marion S. *Gold Diggers and Silver Miners: Prostitution and Social Life on the Comstock Lode.* Ann Arbor: University of Michigan Press. 1981.

Gould, Lewis L. *Wyoming: A Political History, 1868-1896.* New Haven: Yale University Press. 1968.

Gray, James H. *Red Lights on the Prairies.* New York: Signet, New American Library. 1971.

Haller, John S., and Robin M. Haller. *The Physician and Sexuality in Victorian America.* New York: W. W. Norton. 1977

Hegne, Barbara. *Harlots, Hurdies and Spirited Women of Virginia City, Nevada.* Medford: FreeStyle Graphics. 2001.

Hine, Robert V. *The American West: An Interpretive History.* New York: Little Brown. 1973.

Horan, James D. *Desperate Women.* New York: G. P. Putnam's Sons. 1952.

Hunt, Inez, and Wanetta W. Draper. *To Colorado's Restless Ghosts.* Denver: Sage Books. 1960.

Hunter, J. Marvin, editor. *The Trail Drivers of Texas.* Nashville: Cokesbury Press. 1925.

James, Ronald M., and C. Elizabeth Raymond, editors. *Comostock Women: The Making of A Mining Community.* Reno/Las Vegas: University of Nevada Press. 1998.

Keller, George. *A Trip Across the Plains, and Life in California.* Oakland: Biobooks. 1955.

Kessler-Harris, Alice. *Out to Work: A History of Wage-Earning Women in the United States.* New York: Oxford University Press. 1982.

Lamar, Howard R., editor. *The Reader's Encyclopedia of the American West.* New York: Thomas Y. Crowell. 1977.

Lee, Bob, editor. *Gold, Gals, Guns, Guts: A History of Deadwood, Lead, and Spearfish, 1874-1976.* Pierre: South Dakota State Historical Society Press. 2004.

MacKell, Jan. *Brothels, Bordellos, and Bad Girls: Prostitution In Colorado, 1860-1930.* Albuquerque: University of New Mexico Press. 2004.

—————. *Red Light Women of the Rocky Mountains.* Albuquerque: University of New Mexico Press. 2009.

McDonald, Douglas. *The Legend of Julia Bulette and the Red Light Ladies of Nevada*. Las Vegas: Nevada Publications. 1980.

McLoughlin, Denis. *Wild and Woolly: An Encyclopedia of the Old West*. New York: Doubleday & Co. 1975.

Miller, Stuart Creighton. *The Unwelcome Immigrant: The American Image of the Chinese, 1785-1882*. Berkeley: University of California Press. 1969.

O'Neal, Bill. *Encyclopedia of Western Gunfighters*. Norman: University of Oklahoma Press. 1979.

Riley, Glenda. *Inventing the American Woman: An Inclusive History*. Harlan Davidson Inc. 2001.

—————. *The Female Frontier: A Comparative View of Women on the Prairie and the Plains*. Lawrence: University Press of Kansas, 1988.

Riley, Glenda, and Richard W. Etulain, editors. *By Grit and Grace: Eleven Women Who Shaped the American West*. Golden: Fulcrum Publishing. 1997.

—————. *Wild Women of the Old West*. Golden: Fulcrum Publishing. 2003.

Robinson, Charles M., editor. *The Diaries of John C. Bourke, Volume 2: July 29, 1876 – April 7, 1878*. Denton: University of North Texas Press. 2005.

Rosen, Ruth. *The Lost Sisterhood: Prostitution in America, 1900-1918*. Baltimore: Johns Hopkins University Press. 1982.

Rutter, Michael. *Bedside Book of Bad Girls: Outlaw Women of the American West*. Helena: Farcountry Press. 2008.

—————. *Myths and Mysteries of the West*. Guilford and Helena: Two Dot. 2005.

—————. *Outlaw Tales of Utah*. Guilford and Helena: Two Dot. 2nd Edition. 2011.

—————. *Upstairs Girls: Prostitution in the American West*. Helena: Farcountry Press. 2005.

—————. *Wild Bunch Women*. Guilford and Helena: Two Dot. 2003.

Seagraves, Anne. *Soiled Doves: Prostitution in the Early West*. Hayden: Wesanne. 1994.

Selcer, Richard F. *Hell's Half Acre*. Fort Worth: Texas Christian University Press. 1991.

Shannon, William. *The American Irish*. New York: Macmillan. 1963.

Snell, Joseph W. *Painted Ladies of the Cowtown Frontier*. Kansas City: Kansas City Posse of the Westerners. 1965.

Taylor, Lydia Pettengill. *From Under the Lid: An Appeal to True Womanhood*. Portland: Glass & Prudhomme. 1913. PDF ebook.

Tong, Benson. *Unsubmissive Women: Chinese Prostitutes in Nineteenth-Century San Francisco*. Norman and London: University of Oklahoma Press. 1994.

Utley, Robert M. *Frontier Regulars: The United States Army and the Indian, 1866-1891*. New York: Macmillan. 1973.

West, Elliott. *The Saloon on the Rocky Mountain Mining Frontier*. Lincoln: University of Nebraska Press. 1979.

Williams, George, III. *The Red-Light Ladies of Virginia City, Nevada*. Carson City: Tree by the River Publishing. 1984.

—————. *Rosa May: The Search for a Mining Camp Legend*. Carson City: Tree by the River Publishing. 1980.

Wright, Robert Marr. *Dodge City, The Cowboy Capital and the Great Southwest in the Days of the Wild Indian, the Buffalo, the Cowboy, Dance Halls, Gambling Halls and Bad Men*. Wichita: Wichita Eagle Press. 1913.

INDEX

Bold denotes photograph.

brothel in Wyoming, **33**

brothels, vi, 4, **76**; and abuse, 117; in Belle Fourche (SD), 9; and Big Dorothy, 176–177; and children, 20; cost of buying, 135, 140, 164; and Dolly Arthur, 164–165; and Dora DuFran, 5, 10, 11, 13; and Fanny Porter's, 65; and Hall of Mirrors, 136, 140; and Hattie LaPierre, 43; in Helena (MT), 169, 174, 176–178; and Jennie Rogers, 135, 139; and Kitty Leroy, 58; and Mattie Silks, 136; and Mollie Johnson, 123–124, 126; and Molly B'Dam, 101–102; and Palace of Joy, 140; in Portland (OR), 28–29; and racism, 41, 43, 76; and Sadie Orchard, 118, 121; and the Stockade, 82, 84–88, 89–92; in Wyoming, **33**

Burdan (first name unknown), 95

Butte (MT), 32

C

Calamity Jane: alcoholism of, 2–3, 11; Buffalo Bill and, 2–3; character of, 2–3, 11; death of, 11; and Dora DuFran, 11; and feminism, 3; and gambling, 3; myths about, 2, 11; and the press, 2–3, 11–12; and prostitution, 2–3; and Three Mile Hog Ranch, 9; and Wild Bill Hickok, 3

California Gold Rush, 38

Calvington, Leeah. *See* Rogers, Jennie

Camp Floyd, 85

Canary, Martha Jane. *See* Calamity Jane

Carbon County Jail, 107, 109

Carpenter (Judge), 54

Cason, Mabel Earp, 159

Cassidy, Butch: character of, 68; crimes of, 67; and Etta Place, 65, 68; in New York City, 71; in South America, 71, 72; and venereal disease, 69

Central Pacific Railroad, 38

Cheyenne (WY), 33

Cheyenne Club, **69**

Cheyenne Stage Company, 9

Chicago Joe, 174–175

Chinese Exclusion Act, 39

Chinese people: and California Gold Rush, 38; and gambling, 38; and the law, 38, 39, 47; and mining, 41; and opium, 91; and prostitution, 41; and racism, 38, 39, 41, 42; as railroad workers, 38; and slavery, 37, 38, 40

Chinese Poker Bride. *See* Bemis, Polly

Citizens Investment Company, 87

Civic Betterment League, The, 92

Clark, Madam Etta, 117

Cochise (AZ), 150

Colma (CA), 160

Colt revolver, **63**

Comanche Indians: attitudes about, 16–17; camp of, **15**; and kidnapping, 16–17; raids by, 14, 16

Confederacy, 15

Copeland, Thelma Dolly. *See* Arthur, Dolly

Cox, John, 44

Creech, Sarah Jane. *See* Orchard, Sadie

Cummings, Katie. *See* Elder, Kate

Cuny, Adolph, 9

Curley, Samuel: and gambling, 56; marriage to Kitty Leroy, 56; murder/suicide and, 58; reported sightings of his ghost, 61

Custer (SD), 1

Czizek, Jay, 39

D

dance halls and saloons, 36–37, 38, 39, 58, 60, 105, 118, 124, 152, 170

Daughters of Sin, Sisters of Misery, 156–157

De Young's Photo Studios, 71

Deadwood (SD), **125**; Calamity Jane in, 4, 11; Dirty Em in, 4; Dora DuFran in, 4, 5, 9, 13, 123; Ida Cheplan in, 124; Ida Clark in, 124; Jennie Duchesneau in, 124; Jennie Philips in, 124–125; Kitty Leroy in, 56–64; Madame Moustache in, 4; mining in, 1, 11; Mollie Johnson in, 123–129; Molly B'Dam in, 99; Mount Moriah Cemetery (Deadwood, SD) in, 8, 64; prostitution in, 4

Denver (CO), 129, 131–132

Denver (CO), Jennie Rogers in, 135, 139–140

Diddlin' Dora's, 10

Dodge City (KS): Doc Holliday in, 148; Kate Elder in, 143, 148; Libby Thompson in, 19; prostitution laws in, 148–149

Dorothy's Rooms, **171**, 172

Dr. Pierce's Medical Institute, 69

drug abuse: and Harry Black, 49; and hog ranches, 55; and laudanum, v, vi, 33; and Mattie Blaylock, 156, 157, 158; and opium, vi; and Santa Anna, 74, 75, 79; and the Stockade, 91

Dublin, Ireland, 95

duel, 134–135

DuFran, Joseph, 8

DuFran, Madam Dora, **6**; in Belle Fourche (SD), 9; birth of, 4–5, 7; boomtowns and, 4; business practices of, 5; and Calamity Jane, 11; character of, 8; childhood of, 7; death of, 8, 13; generosity of, 5; husband of, 8; marriage of, 8; and Mollie Johnson, 123; myths about, 4; notoriety of, 1; and parrot, 8, 13; in Rapid City (SD), 12

Durgan, Millie, 17

Hickok, Wild Bill, 3, 23
high yellow, 75
Hillsboro (NM), 119
hog ranches (U.S. Army whorehouses), v; Calamity
    Jane and, 11; and drug abuse, 55; and poverty,
    55; and suicide, 55; Three Mile Hog Ranch, 9; and
    tuberculosis, 55; and venereal disease, 55
Holliday, Dr. John "Doc," 23; and gambling, 146, 147,
    148; in Glenwood Springs (CO), 150; and guns,
    142, 148; and Kate Elder, 142, 144, 146–150;
    and stabbing death, 146; and tuberculosis, 148,
    149–150; and Wyatt Earp, 144, 146, 148
Horony, Mary Katherine. *See* Elder, Kate
Horton (Sheriff), 107
Hot Springs (NM), 122
House of Mirrors, 136, 140, **141**
Houston, Sam, 15; and Yellow Rose of Texas myth,
    73; and *Yellow Rose of Texas* song, 81

I
I Married Wyatt Earp, 156, 159–160
influenza, 114

J
Jacksonville (FL), 30
Johnson, Mollie: alleged marriage to black man,
    129; and baseball, 127–128; and buggy race,
    128; business practices of, 123–124, 129; in
    Deadwood (SD), 123–129; and Dora DuFran,
    123; kindness of, 124–126; leaving Deadwood
    (SD), 130; loss of building to fire, 126; myths
    about, 129; possible birth date and place, 130;
    and the press, 126, 129; public exploits of, 124,
    127

K
Kansas, 27
Ketchikan (AK), 161–162, **162**, **163**, 164–168, **165**
Kid Curry: and Annie Rogers, 68, 70–71; capture of,
    71; crimes of, 71; and Fanny Porter's, 70; and the
    Wild Bunch, 70, 71
King, Hong, 36–37, 38, 42, 44
Kingston (NM), 116; as boomtown, 118; Butch
    Cassidy in, 118; Grover Cleveland in, 118; Mark
    Twain in, 118; Sundance Kid in, 118
Kiowa Indians, 17
Klinkhammer, Pete, 47

L
Lake, Stuart, 159
Lakota Sioux, 1
LaPierre, Hattie: arrest and trail, 52, 54; forced into

prostitution, 50–51; in Lander (WY), 50–52;
    pardon of, 54; and physical abuse, 50–51; and
    shooting of husband, 51–52; shot by husband,
    51; in Thermopolis (WY), 49
Last Chance Gulch, 170, 176, 177, 178
laudanum, v, vi, 33, 156, 157
Lay, Marvel, 67
Lead (SD), 5
Leroy, Kitty: arrival in Deadwood, 62; beauty of, 62;
    burial of, 64; character of, 60, 62; as dancer, 56,
    62, 63; and gambling, 56, 58, 60; and guns, 58;
    as madam, 58, 63; marriages of, 56, 60, 62, 63;
    and Mint Gambling Saloon, 58, 63; murder of,
    58; myths about, 56, 60, 62; newspaper article
    about, 56, 59; possible birth date and place, 60;
    reported sightings of her ghost, 61; shooting her
    husband, 62; and trick shooting, 56, 58, 60, 63
Levy, Madam Ivy, 176
Livingston Confectionery, 85
Logan, Harvey. *See* Kid Curry
Lone Star Saloon, 58, 59
Long, Adora. *See* Topham, Dora B.
Longabaugh, Harry. *See* Sundance Kid
Lorunz, Ed, 177
Los Angeles (CA), 152
Low Down on Calamity Jane, 12

M
Madam Belle London. *See* Topham, Dora B.
Madam Dirty Em, 4
Madame Moustache, 4
Marcus, Josephine Sara "Sadie": and acting, 156;
    and Al Sieber, 156–157; and Apache attack,
    156; autobiography of, 156–157, 159–160; and
    Bat Masterson, 153; birth date and place, 156;
    character of, 156–157; death of, 160; early life
    of, 156; education of, 156; and gambling, 160;
    and *I Married Wyatt Earp*, 156, 159–160; and
    John Behan, 156–157; in Prescott, AZ, 156; and
    the press, 159; professional names of, 153; as
    prostitute, 157; and Wyatt Earp, 152–153, 156,
    158–160
Martin, Councilman L. D., 86, **86**
Masterson, Bat, 23, 153
McKinney, Frank. *See* Black, Harry H.
McLaury, Frank, 158
McLaury, Tom, 158
McMicken (first name unknown), 107
mercury, 108, 109
Michaels, Katharine (or Katherine). *See* Elder, Kate
Miles City (MT), 5
miners and mining: and Apache attacks, 119;

and boomtowns, 166; and Chinese people, 47; in Colorado, 24, 135; conditions of, 47; in Deadwood (SD), 1, 4, 9, 130; in Encampment, WY, 107; in Helena (MT), 172; in Ketchikan (AK), 161, 167; in Kingston (NM), 116, 118; in Murray (ID), 99, 101–102; and prostitution, 62, 118–119; Solitaire mine, 118

Minnesota, 31

Mint Gambling Saloon, 63; and Kitty Leroy, 58

Molly B'Dam: birth date and place, 95; in blizzard, 100; business practices of, 94, 102; and Calamity Jane, 99; Catholic religion of, 95, 98, 99, 101; character of, 94–95, 101; childhood of, 95; in Deadwood (SD), 99; death of, 104; description of, 95; education of, 95; and "erotic baths," 102; excommunication from Catholic Church, 99; grave marker of, **103**; introduction into prostitution, 98; kindness of, 100–101, 102; as madam, 102; marriage of, 95; in Murray (ID), 99, 101–104; myths about, 94, 99, 101; in New York City, 95; origin of name, 101; popularity of, 101; rescue of woman and child, 100; and smallpox epidemic, 102; and tuberculosis, 104

"Molly B'Dam Gold Rush Days," 104

Morgan, Emily West: beauty of, 73, 74, 76; education of, 75–76, 78; freeborn papers of, **77**; freeborn status of, 75, 76; as indentured servant, 76, 78; and James Morgan, 76; racial heritage of, 73, 74–75; return to New England, 79; and slavery, 76; and Yellow Rose of Texas myth, 73–75, 79, 81

Morgan, James: as businessman, 78; and Emily West, 76; and slavery, 78; and Yellow Rose of Texas myth, 79, 81

Mormons: and prostitution, 84–85; and the Stockade, 82, 91

Morris, Otis, 39

Mount Moriah Cemetery (Deadwood, SD), 8, 64

Murray (ID), 99, **100**, 101–104

N

Nathoy, LaLu. *See* Bemis, Polly

Nation, Carrie, **93**

New Washington (TX), 73, 78

New York Daily News, 40

New York (NY): Etta Place in, 69; Molly B'Dam in, 95; Sundance Kid in, 69; the Wild Bunch in, 71

New York Times, 155

newspaper reporting, 126–127

O

Ocean Grove Hotel, **120**, 121

Ogden (UT), 82, 85, 93

opium, 74, 75, 91

Orchard, James W., 119

Orchard, Sadie, **113**, **120**; birth of, 116; business practices of, 114, 115, 118–119, 120, 121; character of, 112, 114, 118; childhood of, 112, 116; civic involvement of, 112; death of, 122; description of, 115; divorce of, 115, 121; education of, 112, 116; grave marker of, 116; and guns, 114; in Hillsboro, NM, 114, 119; as horsewoman, 114; and hotel business, 121; and influenza epidemic, 114; kindness of, 114; in Kingston (NM), 116, 118; and the law, 115; marriage of, 119; myths about, 116, 118, 120; shooting at husband, 114–115; and stagecoach business, 120; and syphilis, 122; and Victorian style, 119, 121

Orchard-Matthewson Stage Line, 119–120

O'Rourke, Phil, 101, 103

P

Page Act, 38

Palace Ballard Hall, 85

Palace of Joy, 140

Parker, Cynthia Ann, 17

Parker, Quanah, 17

Passwater, James E., 105–107, 109

Patterson, Eleanor. *See* Gizycka, Eleanor

Peterson, Louis, 106

Philips, Jennie, 124–126

Pinkerton Agency, 71, 72

Pinkerton Agency, and the Wild Bunch, 67

Place, Etta: beauty of, 65; and Butch Cassidy, 68; character of, 67, 68; as criminal, 68; description of, 67; and guns, 68; and Mormon family, 67; myths about, 65, 72; in New York City, 69; portrait photos of, 71; possible birth date and place, 67; real first name of, 67; in South America, 71, 72; and Sundance Kid, 65, **66**, 67, 68, 69; and venereal disease, 69; and the Wild Bunch, 67, 68

Poker Bride. *See* Bemis, Polly

Poker Game Bride legend, 36–37, 39

Portland (OR): and Floating Brothel, 28–29; Polly Bemis in, 37, 40, 44

Prescott (AZ), 156

prison doors, **110**

Prohibition, 12, 165, 167, 173

prostitutes, **vii**, **53**; and abortion, 20; and birth control, 20; child of, **21**; children of, 20; myths about, viii; professional names of, 135, 142, 172; racial mix of, 91; and suicide, v;

typical dress of, 115; writings by, 12, 25–27, 30, 32–33, 34, 156, 159

prostitution: and boomtowns, vii, 1, 62, 166–167; and child abuse, 26, 30–32; and drug abuse, v, vi, 33; economics of, viii, 28–29, 37, 40, 42, 43, 44, 57, 84–85, 87, 90, 91, 115, 117, 139, 163, 166–167; euphemisms for, 173–174; and feminism, 26, 32 ; and gambling, 58, 60, 62–63; and guns, 50–51, 114–115, 134–135; and health care, 88–89; in Ketchikan (AK), 165–168; and the law, vii, 28–29, 43, 82, 84–85, 91, 92, 115, 117, 119, 140, 148, 161, 162, 166–167, 168, 173, 176–177; and miners, 62, 118–119; and morality, vii, viii, 26, 35, 84, 88–89, 98, 161, 173; and Mormons, 82, 84; myths about, 36–37, 134–135; and politics, 82, 85, 87, 88, 119, 139–140, 173, 176–177; and poverty, 33; and the press, 37, 39, 43, 126–127, 173; and Prohibition, 12, 93, 165, 173; and racism, 26, 38, 43, 129; and rape, 51; and religion, 26, 32, 98; and slavery, 16, 37, 40–41, 44, 50–51, 78; societal attitudes about, v, vi, vii, viii, 20, 26; and Three Mile Hog Ranch, 9, 55; and the U.S. Army, 55, 85, 96–97; and venereal disease, vi, 88–89, 91, 97, 108, 109, 118; working conditions of, 91, 117

Putnam, Dorothy. See Big Dorothy

Q

Quayle, William, 140

Queen of the Blondes, The. See Johnson, Mollie

Queen of the Colorado Underworld. See Rogers, Jennie

Queen of the Underworld, The. See Rogers, Jennie

R

racism, 26, 38, 43, 129

Rapid City (SD), 5; Dora DuFran in, 12; flood in, 13

Rawlins (WY), 54

Ready, Jack "Handsome Jack," 137

red light districts, viii, 84, 126, 155, 161, **165**, 167, 173

Redwater River, 9

Republic of Texas, 15

Rocky Mountain News, 140

Rogers, Annie, 68; arrest of, 71; beauty of, 70–71; and Kid Curry, 68, 70–71, **70**

Rogers, Jennie, **133**; attempted murder charge and, 132; birth date and place, 132; and blackmail, 140; and Bright's Disease, 140; business practices of, 134–135, 139–141; in Chicago, 141; death of, 141; death of husband, 132; in Denver (CO), 131–132, 135, 139–140;

description of, 132; early life of, 132, 134; and guns, 132; and high-end brothels, 135, 139–140; and horses, 131; and House of Mirrors, 140; investments of, 139; marriages of, 132, 134, 141; and politics, 139–140; and the press, 140; in Salt Lake City (UT), 131–132; shooting boyfriend, 132; swindled by husband, 141; violent temper of, 132

S

Salmon River, 42, 45, **47**, 48

saloons and dance halls, 36–37, 38, 39, 58, 60, 105, 118, 124, 152, 170

Salt Lake City Council, 84

Salt Lake City (UT): Dora Topham in, 82, 87–93; Jennie Rogers in, 131–132

Salt Lake Security and Trust Company, 87

San Antonio (TX), 65

San Francisco (CA), 37, 44

Santa Anna, **74**; and Emily West, 78–79; and Yellow Rose of Texas myth, 73–75

sexually transmitted diseases. See venereal disease

Shepp, Charlie, 47

Silks, Mattie, **136**, **138**; business practices of, 136, 138; death of, 137; early life of, 137; and House of Mirrors, **136**; and Jennie Rogers, **136**; marriage of, 137; and politics, 136–137; swindled by boyfriends, 137; wealth of, 136

sin districts. See red light districts

Sioux Indians, 1, 4

slavery, 15, 16, 37, 40–41, 44, 76, 78

smallpox, 102

Smith, Taylor, 39

Solitaire mine, 118

Spencer, Lew, 129

Squirrel Tooth Alice. See Thompson, Libby

Stockade, the: business practices at, 87; daily life in, 91; decline and closure of, 92; description of, 87; economics of, 84; health care in, 89, 91; and the law, 84, 91; and Mormons, 85, 91; opium in, 91; other businesses in, 91; and politics, 87; proposal for, 82; public opinion and, 90, 92; racial backgrounds of workers in, 91; recruiting for, 90; as red light district, 82; security at, 91; underage boy in, 91–92

Stone House, 51

Sturgis (SD), 5

Sundance Kid, **66**

Sundance Kid, the: character of, 68; crimes of, 67; and Etta Place, 65, 67, 68, 69; in New York City, 71; in South America, 71, 72; and venereal disease, 69

ABOUT THE AUTHOR

Michael Rutter has authored or co-authored forty books and text-books—and written over 700 articles for magazines, journals, and newspapers. His most recent publications include *Upstairs Girls: Prostitution in the American West, Bedside Book of Bad Girls: Outlaw Women of the American West, Wild Bunch Women,* and *Outlaw Tales of Utah.* Michael is a passionate historian and a devoted outdoorsman. He is also an award-winning author, having won the Ben Franklin Award for Outdoor Writing and also the Rocky Mountain Book Publishers Award. Recently, his essay on fly fishing placed first in a writing contest at Yale University. In the summer, he travels extensively around the western United States doing research. He lives in Orem, Utah, with his wife, Shari, two cats, and a spoiled Turkish Akbash named Starrfish. In the winter, he teaches advanced writing at Brigham Young University.